The Evolution of Law

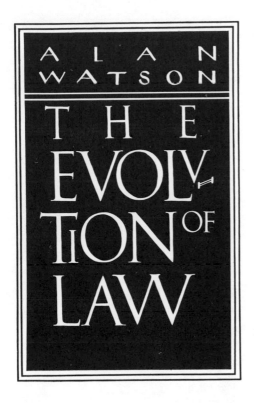

ALAN WATSON

THE EVOLUTION OF LAW

THE JOHNS HOPKINS UNIVERSITY PRESS

BALTIMORE, MARYLAND

© 1985 The Johns Hopkins University Press
All rights reserved
Printed in the United States of America

The Johns Hopkins University Press, 701 West 40th Street,
Baltimore, Maryland 21211

The paper in this book is acid-free and meets the
guidelines for permanence and durability of the
Committee on Production Guidelines for Book
Longevity of the Council on Library Resources.

Photographs on pp. ii and 2 are reprinted courtesy of
the Bibliothèque Nationale, Paris. For descriptive
information, see p. 121.

**Library of Congress Cataloging
in Publication Data**

Watson, Alan.
    The evolution of law.

    Includes bibliographical references and index.
    1. Law—History and criticism.   2. Roman law—
History.   I. Title.
K150.W37   1985   340'.09   84-21835
ISBN 0-8018-2504-0

For Esen

Contents

Preface

In this book I seek to present a general and coherent view of the nature of legal change which is independent of a particular time and place. I wish to explain why and how law changes in mature systems, in underdeveloped systems, and in legal systems, even of different levels of sophistication and from different societal roots, that come into powerful contact. I hope and intend that the information I give, my arguments, and my conclusions will be useful tools for everyone interested in law and society, whether as legal historians (of any country or period), sociologists of law, anthropologists, or law reformers. I am well aware that in every chapter my conclusions are radical and will appear so especially to scholars who adopt conventional, even Marxist, approaches to law in society. Yet this originality must be made explicit because, almost paradoxically, the conclusions seem to follow so simply from the evidence that they may appear all too obvious and even banal to the uninitiated in legal theory. As will appear, I believe passionately that any general theory of legal development must be grounded in actual historical data, observed as dispassionately as possible and considered comparatively. Hence come the individual, disparate themes of each chapter. For my goals to be satisfied, specialists in the field covered by each chapter must be convinced that my scholarship is sound and my particular conclusions plausible; and non-specialists must be able to follow my arguments and believe that my conclusions can be generalized. The message of each chapter is wider than might at first appear. The opening chapter concentrates on the evolution of Roman contract law, but my intention is not only to contribute to our understanding of Roman law but, more importantly, to throw a spotlight on the general force of the legal tradition on the growth of law within a mature legal system. The most original and admired part of the most innovative legal system is used here to demonstrate the blindness of the legal elite to other societal concerns. The second half of the chapter is devoted to showing, by other instances, that the impact of the legal tradition on legal evolution is also enormous in other lands and in other contexts, and that the conclusions from Roman contract law can be generalized. The chapter on customary law is intended on the primary level to show how customary law has developed in, and is related to, Western European society (particularly in the Middle Ages), but the findings also explain the nature of customary law everywhere. Customary law is typically misunderstood; hence, theory is prominent in this chapter. A further implication is that this misunderstanding of the real nature of customary law has led to many fundamental problems in legal history. The chapter on the Reception of Roman law is intended to provide a general answer to what has been called the most momentous and puzzling problem in history. By building on generalizations that can be extracted from the preceding chapters and by examining similar massive borrowings of law, my aim is even more to further understanding of the relationship between law and the society in which it operates, and of the vital role played by legal transplants in legal growth. In the next chapter, Sir George Mackenzie's defense of Haining is first examined as one example of how the themes of the three preceding chapters converge in law in action. But the case also reveals that one cannot understand how law operates in society and how it changes if the factors set out in the earlier chapters are ignored. Finally it is argued that even during legal or social revolution, the legal tradition survives or is replaced in whole or in part by another legal tradition.

The portion of Chapter 1 dealing with the evolution of Roman contract law was delivered as a lecture in the Department of Legal History of the University of Glasgow and in the Jurisprudence and Social Policy Program of the University of California at Berkeley; and a version was published in *Law and History Review* (1984). Likewise, part of Chapter 2 was published in the Legal History Symposium issue of the *Illinois Law Review* (1984). A shortened version of Chapter 3 was presented at "From Late Antiquity to Early Islam," a meeting at Princeton in March 1984. To all who have given me criticism I am very grateful and above all to Steve Burbank, John Ford, and Michael Hoeflich, who read all or most of my manuscript at least once.

Because some of the terms may be unfamiliar, I have appended a glossary.

The Evolution of Law

I

The Roman System of Contracts and the Legal Tradition

I hope to show in this book that one cannot understand legal development in general without a new look at the history of individual legal changes and that, in turn, a new approach to legal development in general can lead to a more just appreciation of individual legal changes. My technique is to analyze particular legal events and facts, show that they have a significance beyond their immediate context, and generalize from them in order to construct a picture of how law evolves.

I have two aims in the first and main part of this chapter. First, I wish to add to our knowledge of the history of Roman law by producing a radically different view of the development of contracts that is, I believe, both consistent with the surviving textual data and plausible with regard to human behavior. Second, I wish to contribute to our general understanding of how and why law develops when it does develop, and explain the evolution of some very familiar legal institutions. I cannot accomplish the second aim without accomplishing the first. Little need be said about the importance of the subject. Subsequently in the chapter I will give a few, relatively random instances to show that one can generalize from Roman contract law to claim that the impact of the legal tradition on legal change is enormous.[1]

Roman Contract Law

Roman law has been the most innovative and most copied system in the West: the law of contract was the most original part of that system and the most admired. Private agreements and the relevant law occupy a central role in mercantile countries—indeed, in the Western world in general—and one would expect on a priori grounds that a particularly vivid light would be cast by this branch of law on the whole subject of legal development and of law in society. This should be the more true in that a contract is a private agreement, almost a private law, operating, say, between two individuals, but it requires state recognition. The state may be slow or quick to give such recognition: slow, as in England, where, by the late twelfth century, the king's court exercised much jurisdiction over property law and criminal law but little over contract;[2] quick, as at Rome, where, before 451 B.C., *stipulatio* could be used to make a legally enforceable agreement. The state may also have reservations about recognizing private agreements. It may restrict its recognition to agreements involving a specified minimum value, only those being considered to have sufficient social or economic consequences to interest the state. Or it may restrict its recognition to agreements concluded with specified formalities, the implication being that formalities could constitute evidence for others or bring home to the parties the significance of what they were doing, and that only parties sufficiently serious to make use of the formalities deserve to have recognition of their agreement by the state. Or it may restrict its recognition to agreements on a particular subject matter—for instance, as at Rome, an agreement to exchange goods for money but not an agreement to exchange goods for services. Or the state recognition may involve various combinations of these restrictions: for instance, the French *Code Civil*, article 1341, provides that (apart from specific exceptions) any agreement above a very tiny sum, although it is valid as a contract, is not susceptible of proof in court unless there is a written document either accepted by a notary or signed by the parties; and the German *Bürgerliches Gesetzbuch,* section 518, requires for recognition of a gift-agreement that it be recorded judicially or notarially.

The immediate thrust of the present chapter is to account for the recognition by the Roman state of the individual types of contract, such as deposit and sale; to show why they arose individually in the chronological order that they did; to indicate why the dividing lines between one contract and another are as they are; and to explain why other contracts, such as a general contract in writing, did not arise or, as in the case of barter, arose only late and with unsatisfactory rules. It will become apparent that, though economic or social reasons demanded the introduction of each type, it was the legal tradition that determined the nature, structure, and chronology of every contract. The basic structure of Roman contract law then remained, long after there was any societal justification for the divisions.

This inquiry begins with the era shortly before the enactment of the Twelve Tables, the earliest Roman codification, which is traditionally and, I think, accurately attributed to around 451–450 B.C.[3] For present purposes I will tentatively define *contract* as an agreement between two or more persons whose main legal consequence is an obligation with an effect personal rather than real. In any investigation of a legal system from a very different time and place there is, of course, always an initial difficulty of categorization. Specifically, here the question is whether the Romans of that time conceived the notion of contract as we do. The answer is probably no, that in fact the Romans had then no abstract concept of "contract." The tentative definition includes, of the institutions existing in the early fifth century B.C., the contract of *stipulatio,* but it excludes conveyances like *mancipatio* and *in jure cessio* and security transactions like *nexum,* even though these include elements of obligation based on agreement.[4] This separation may seem unfortunate. But there are three grounds for accepting the tentative definition. First, our knowledge of the structure of the Twelve Tables is limited, and we have no evidence that the early Romans would have classified stipulatio with mancipatio and the others. Second, the tentative definition allows us to include all the obligations that the later Romans regarded as contractual, and to exclude all the obligations that the later Romans did not regard as contracts. Third, the modern perspective that is enshrined in the definition is a continuation of the ideas that the Romans came to develop.

It is often said that the Romans never developed a system of contract but only individual contracts,[5] and the attempt is sometimes made to explain in economic terms why each contract arose when it did. Such attempts are doomed to failure. No investigation into contracts one by one and separately can make sense in economic terms of the order of their appearance. For instance, deposit appears in the fifth century B.C., loan for consumption in the third century B.C. at the latest, but barter, insofar as it ever was a contract at all, had to wait at least another few hundred years; and all this while there was no contract of sale until about 200 B.C. Again, there was no specific contract for reward for looking after a thing, reward in return for another's use of one's thing, or reward for one's services until, after the advent of coined money, the introduction of the contract of hire sometime close to 200 B.C. In these circumstances, the early dating, before 123 B.C.,[6] of the invention of a contract of mandate where someone agreed to act gratuitously for another—and the essence of the contract was specifically that the performance was to be gratuitous—seems unlikely if the need for the contract is to be explained on economic grounds.

The truth is more complicated, but if one is prepared to grant legal tradition an important role in legal development, then the unfolding of the growth of Roman contracts is rational and simple to explain. The starting point is that from very early times the Romans did have a method—the stipulatio in fact—by which parties could agree to create any obligation which was not positively unlawful. If one dares to speak probably anachronistically, one can say that in very early times the Romans did have a general theory of contract, not a law of individual contracts. The question to be resolved then is how this general approach to contract came to be lost. The clue to the development lies in a very strange fact that needs an explanation: apart from the very special and complex case of partnership, all Roman contracts either have a money prestation or no prestation. In this latter category are two kinds of contract: they may either be gratuitous of necessity or they are unilateral (in which case they may be matched with another contract). What does not exist, apart from that late and uncertain instance of barter, is a Roman contract where goods or services are proffered in return for goods or services. What is striking, moreover, is that in deciding which contract is involved, the touchstone is whether performance is necessarily (so far as the contract goes) for nothing or whether the performance is for money. For instance, the three distinct contracts of *depositum*, *commodatum* (loan for use) and *mandatum* all become hire (*locatio conductio*) if payment is promised. What is so significant about a prestation in coined money that a Roman contractual type must either contain it or be gratuitous? The solution to the problem of development, I submit, is that in most cases an individual type of Roman contract arose subsequently to stipulatio when, for whatever reason, a stipulatio was inappropriate or inefficient for that type of situation and when there was a societal need. Thus, almost every subsequent contractual type is a derogation from stipulatio. It should be noted that a legal remedy on an agreement is needed, not in accordance with the frequency of important transactions, but in accordance with the frequency of their going wrong.

The origins of the stipulatio (also known as the *sponsio*) are obscure, and may have involved a libation or an oath, but they need not concern us now, nor should further conclusions be drawn from any hypothesis as to origins.[7] What matters is that it was well-developed before the time of the Twelve Tables, under which the contract was actionable by the form of process known as *legis actio per iudicis postulationem* (G.4.17a). It was a formal, unilateral contract in which the promisee asked, "Do you promise [whatever it might be]?" necessarily using the verb *spondere* and the promisor immediately replied "*Spondeo*," "I promise," using the same verb. Later other verbs could be used, but *spondere* could only be used by Roman citizens. The content of the promise was judged only by the words used, and the contract would remain valid and effective even if the promise was induced by fraud, was extorted by fear, or proceeded on an error. Stipulatio could be used for any lawful purpose: to promise a dowry, make a sale (when mutual stipulationes would be needed), engage one's services,[8] and so on. But when an agreement was not cast in the form of a stipulation, then, no matter how serious the intentions of the parties, no matter how important the subject matter of the transaction, there was no contractual obligation and no right to any disappointed party to bring a contractual action.

Stipulatio, by skillful modernization, could have become the root of a flexible, unitary contractual system. Writing, perhaps incorporated into two documents, could have been adopted as an alternative to the oral question and answer, or agreement (however it was proved), could have become the basis of a contract; remedies for fraud, intimidation, or error could have been made inherent in the contract; and implied terms could have been developed for specific types of factual situation. Instead, a number of other individual contracts arose, each defined in terms of its function. This definition by function and not by form separates them sharply from stipulation. They might even appear to be lesser breeds, particular rather than general. Each of the contractual arrangements, however, whether loan for consumption or sale, could be cast in the form of one or more stipulationes and then would be that type of contract.

One early contract was *mutuum,* loan for consumption. Mutuum was provided with the rather strange action known as the *condictio,* which lay when the plaintiff claimed that the defendant owned a thing which he was legally bound to deliver to the plaintiff. Many scholars believe mutuum to be very old, with a prehistory before it came to be provided with the condictio—and if so, the general argument of this chapter is strengthened—but much that is peculiar about the condictio is explicable, as we shall see, if we link the introduction of that action with the creation of mutuum as a legal institution. The form of action, the *legis actio per condictionem*, was introduced by the *lex Silia* when what was claimed was a determinate sum of money, by the *lex Calpurnia* when what was claimed was a definite thing (G.4.19). It is usually held that the *lex Silia* was earlier, on the basis that otherwise there would be no need for a law specifically covering money.[9] David Daube, as we shall see, adds a new dimension. In any event, whatever the priority of these two statutes may have been, the remedy of the condictio is old. As early as the composition of the *Rudens* by Plautus, who died in 184 B.C., the classical procedure by *formula* could be used for the condictio as well as the archaic procedure by *legis actio*.[10] And there would be little point in setting up fresh legis actiones once formulae were in being.

The peculiarities of the condictio are that it is abstract in the sense that the plaintiff does not set out in the pleadings the grounds of his case; that it is general in that it can be brought any time a nonowner believes that the owner of money or of a certain thing is under a legal obligation to give it him;[11] and that, apart from exceptional cases, there had to be a preceding delivery of the thing to the defendant by the plaintiff. Thus, the condictio could be brought both where there was and where there was not a contract.[12] The generality coupled with the abstraction requires explanation, and the simplest explanation is that the condictio was originally envisaged for one concrete situation which was so obvious that it did not have to be expressly set out—and then was found to be extendable to others. The most obvious concrete situation is mutuum, which in fact has always been treated as the primary use of the condictio. Loan for consumption would need to be given legal effectiveness when there was a breakdown in neighborly relations, when one friend failed to repay a loan: in an early agricultural community a loan of seed corn to be repaid after the harvest would be a common case. No stipulation would have been taken precisely because it is morally inappropriate for one friend, performing an amicable service, to demand a formal contract from another.[13] Where the loan was commercial, a stipulation would have been taken, to cover interest as well, and there would be no need for a specific contract of mutuum. We now see also why the action on mutuum was for the principal only, and did not extend to interest: friends do not demand interest from friends.[14] The breakdown in neighborly relations might be related to an increase in Rome's size.

But the earliest action for a mutuum was apparently for money, not for seed corn. This is explained by David Daube in a wide framework. He stresses that "some transactions, originally belonging to the gift area of fellowship, 'Gemeinschaft,' tend to assume the more rigid, legalistic characteristics of partnership, 'Gesellschaft,' when money enters." Specifically with regard to mutuum, the giving of an action—at first restricted to a money loan—marks for him a breakdown in the gift trade.[15] Earlier, a gift of corn or money to a friend in need was expected to be returned by a converse gift at an opportune time. I would prefer to think that even before the *lex Silia*, the idea in mutuum was that of a loan to be returned in due course, but that is a minor matter. What is significant is that Daube offers a plausible explanation for the condictio's being originally restricted to a claim for money.

Another early specific type of contract, I believe, was deposit. The jurist Paul tells us: "On account of deposit an action is given by the Twelve Tables for double, by the praetor's edict for single."[16] It has long been held—by me as well as by others—that the action for double under the Twelve Tables, being penal, was not necessarily based on any concept of contract and was closer to delict,[17] and the further suggestion is then sometimes made that the delict is akin to theft.[18] But what must be stressed at this point is the very restricted scope of the action. It lies, if we believe Paul, where a thing that was deposited is not returned: according to Paul's words, it does not lie, nor does any similar ancient action we know of, where a thing that was hired out or was lent for use is not returned, nor even, deposit being necessarily gratuitous, where a fee was to be paid for looking after the property. Moreover, apart from questions of contract, there seems little need for the action. The owner would have the normal action (of the time) claiming ownership, the *legis actio sacramento in rem*, and he would have the action for theft at least if the depositee moved the thing (and it would be of little use to him if he did not). There seems little reason to single out this particular situation for a specific action based on the notion of delict.

What then would impel the desire for a specific action? Deposit differs from hire of a thing and loan for use firstly in that the object deposited is being taken out of circulation—no one can use it, and certainly not the depositee, since the contract is definitely not for the benefit of the depositee—and secondly in that it is precisely the recipient who is bestowing the favor. It follows that the depositor is in no position to demand that the recipient formally promise by contract to restore the thing: the depositor cannot reward the depositee for his good deed by showing doubts about his honesty. Again, the reason the depositor is willing to have his property out of circulation for a time is often that he finds himself in an emergency and cannot look after the property himself—as a result of earthquake, fire, collapse of a building, or shipwreck—and here too, he is in no position to demand the formality of a stipulation from his helper. But the depositor is particularly vulnerable to fraud, and it is reasonable to give him a forceful remedy with penal damages. In the late Republic, the praetor issued a complicated edict on deposit[19] whose main clauses gave an action for double damages against a depositee who failed to return property entrusted to him in what has come to be called *depositum miserabile*—deposit made as a result of earthquake, fire, collapse of a building, or shipwreck—and an action for simple damages in other cases. Arguments have been produced both for the proposition that the Twelve Tables' provision applied only to depositum miserabile[20] and also for the proposition that it applied to deposits of all kinds. The arguments seem inconclusive, though I tend to favor the second and more usual view, but in either eventuality the argument given here for an early specific action in fraud would fit. The strength of feeling that the depositor should have an action in the event of fraud would be intensified if, as seems likely, deposits were frequently made in temples or with priests (cf., e.g., Plautus, *Bacchides*, 306).

One of the great Roman inventions—it is now widely accepted that there were no foreign models[21]—is the consensual contract, a contract which is legally binding simply because of the parties' agreement and which requires no formalities for its formation. There were four of these, and it is generally presumed that the contract of sale, *emptio venditio*, was the earliest. It seems to me to have been fully actionable by around 200 B.C.[22] There have been numerous theories to explain the origins of consensual sale.[23] Some of these, such as the hypothesis that at one time the agreement became binding only if the buyer had given the seller an earnest of his payment of the price, or only if the seller had delivered to the buyer, are now seen to lack support from the sources. Others, such as that of Theodor Mommsen that state contracts (for example, the public sale of booty) provided the example or model,[24] are concerned with the issue of what gave the Romans the idea that agreements without formality might be actionable, but provide no other insight into the transformation of private bargains into contracts of sale which, though made by private individuals, were enforced by the courts. There may be more than one root in the development of the consensual contract. But whatever economic or social pressures one wants to postulate, whether one says consensual sale was wanted because (as some think) of an expansion of foreign trade and the need for contracts that could be made at a distance, or because (as others hold) of a need for a formless contract to accommodate foreign merchants unfamiliar with Roman law formalities, or because (as still others argue) of a growing awareness of the worth of good faith in contract law for dealings with both Romans and foreigners,[25] the same conclusion holds: consensual sale as a separate contract arose in part because of the inadequacy of the stipulatio for the task. Of one thing there should be no doubt. Before the introduction of the consensual contract, parties to a sale-type transaction who wanted legal enforcement of their agreement would make their arrangements in the form of stipulations.[26] And further development would not have occurred if this way of making arrangement had been satisfactory.

My own version of the origins of consensual sale and the connection with stipulatio[27] derives from the observation of two defects in the contract of sale which were there initially and continued to exist for centuries, namely that the contract did not contain any inherent warranty of title or against eviction nor any inherent warranty against latent defects. Yet buyers did want the protection of warranties, as hundreds of texts on the actual taking of warranties by stipulatio show. And the notion of inherent warranties was not foreign to Roman lawyers because they had already existed for centuries in the *mancipatio,* the formal method of transferring certain types of important property. The absence of inherent warranties would make the consensual contract far less valuable commercially. Whenever merchants wanted warranties—and the evidence shows that they often did—the parties had to be face-to-face to take a stipulation: hence, the contract could not be made by letter or by messenger. Certainly, one could send a dependent member of one's family to take or give the stipulation but that in itself would often be inconvenient and expensive.[28] The absence of inherent warranties for centuries, the strong Roman desire for warranties, and their knowledge that warranties could be implied, demand an explanation which I believe can be found only if we postulate an

origin for the contract where the deficiencies were not so obvious.[29]

If we go back beyond the origin of sale, the parties to a salelike
arrangement who wished a legally binding agreement would, as
I have said, conclude their business by stipulations. They had no
alternative. All terms, given the nature of stipulatio, would have
to be spelled out. The buyer would promise payment on a fixed
date, with interest if he delayed. The seller would promise that he
would deliver the thing on a fixed day, that he would pay a
penalty if he delayed, that the buyer would not be evicted from
the thing, and that the thing was free from hidden defects. Each
stipulatio was unilateral, but the parties would want their rights
and duties to be reciprocal: hence the obligation to fulfill each
stipulatio would have to be made conditional upon the fulfill-
ment, or the readiness to fulfill, of the other. To make matters
worse, this conditional reciprocity would have to be framed so as
to take account of a partial but not complete failure to perform.
For instance, if a sold slave was found to be suffering from some
relatively unimportant defect, the buyer might still want to have
the slave but pay only a reduced price. The drafting and taking of
the stipulations would be extremely cumbrous and complex, and
often it would happen that the parties' intentions would be
frustrated. So far we are on sure ground. What follows is a
conjectural, but I think plausible, account of how the praetor, the
magistrate in charge of the law courts, dealt with the problem. At
some point a praetor accepted that he ought to grant an action in
accordance with good faith to cover accidental interstices in
stipulations concerned with a sale.[30] Above all he would seek to
make the obligations reciprocal. In accordance with the Roman
tendency to see law in terms of blocks,[31] the strict law stipulatio
and the new action based on good faith would be kept separate.
But the position would be reached that provided there was a
sale-type situation and at least one stipulatio, there would be an
action to give the buyer or the seller an action against the other
for an amount equal to what ought to be given or done in

accordance with good faith. The separate contract of sale was in process of being born. But what would be the content of the necessary stipulation? In the simplest possible sale-type transaction there would be, immediately upon agreement, a handing over of the money and a handing over of the thing. The stipulation wanted would cover only continuing obligations, and they would be only of the seller and would consist only of a warranty against eviction and against latent defects. We know from the republican writer Varro (*De re rustica* 2.2.4; 2.3.4; 2.4.5) that these warranties were contained in a single stipulation. Eventually, an action on *emptio venditio* would be given even when no stipulation was taken, but because of the way the contract emerged, it long provided no remedy if the buyer suffered eviction or the object contained hidden defects, so long as the seller was in good faith. Heavy stress is placed on good faith in *emptio venditio* whether as a result of the way the contract emerged or, as many think, as part of the pressure for recognizing the contract. This suggested development has one further feature that renders it plausible. It avoids any sudden leap forward in legal thinking: it is bedded firmly on how parties to a sale-type transaction would conduct their business, and the gradual response of those in charge of lawmaking to the problems that arose.[32]

A second consensual contract, hire (*locatio conductio*), has more obscure origins, but the usual assumption is that its beginnings are closely connected with those of sale and that sale was the more important case: either the example of sale was followed for hire, which is thus a later contract, or the impetus for recognizing a contract of sale impelled also, and simultaneously, the recognition of the less significant locatio conductio. The need to attach legal importance to good faith in contracts would, for instance, be one joint impelling factor.[33] If one grants priority to sale, whether in time or in legal importance, then one fact emerges unequivocally for hire, though strangely it appears never to have been noticed either by Romans or by later scholars. Locatio conductio is a residual category for all types of bilateral agree-ment that are not sale and where the prestation of one of the parties has to be in money. This and this alone can account for the peculiarity that at least three very different contractual situa-tions are included within it: the use of a thing for a time in return for money; providing one's labor for a time in return for money; and the assignment of a specific task to be performed in return for money. In each of these situations the obligations of the party who is acting in return for money are very different. Any doubts that locatio conductio is a residual category must disappear when one notices that in the corresponding situations where no money is to change hands, this one contract is replaced by three: mandate, deposit, and loan for use.[34] It is in the highest degree illuminating for the force of legal tradition in legal development that such a figure as locatio conductio came into being, remained unchanged in its scope throughout the Roman period, and still flourishes in some countries, such as France, Chile, and Ar-gentina, as one contract today.

As a further indication that one need not, even within the Western tradition, draw the line between one type of contract and another exactly as it usually is drawn, it is worth observing that in the second century B.C. at Rome, an agreement to allow another to pasture his flock on one's land for the winter in return for a money payment was regarded as sale of the fodder (Cato, *De agri cultura* 149). Classical Roman and modern law would treat the agreement as hire. The republican position was perfectly sensible and would have remained so in classical law, given the fact that sale did not involve a requirement to transfer ownership but only to give quiet possession—in this case for the duration of the agreement. The standard warranties in sale against eviction and hidden defects would have been perfectly appropriate.

A third consensual contract, mandate (*mandatum*), was in existence by 123 B.C.[35] and is different in its *raison d'être* from the two just examined. Mandate is the agreement to perform gratu-itously a service for another. It is thus not a commercial contract, but an agreement among friends. It is thus again precisely the type of situation where a stipulation could not be demanded; either from the friend who was asked to perform the service or by the friend for repayment of his expenses. That the contract came into existence at all is a tribute to the great weight that the Romans placed upon friendship: friends were expected to do a great deal for one another. It may seem surprising that such a distinction is made between agreeing to act gratuitously for another and acting for reward, but the Roman attitude that found labor degrading is probably a sufficient explanation. It is that, at least, that led to the view that performance of *artes liberales* could not be the subject of locatio conductio.[36]

A similar explanation can account for the emergence of *commodatum*, a gratuitous loan for use, as a separate contract, probably around the beginning of the first century B.C.:[37] one friend who lends gratuitously to a friend cannot demand a formal promise for return. The same holds for the remodeled obligation of deposit probably around the same date.

The origins of *pignus*, pledge, as an individual contract are not so easily uncovered. As a real security transaction giving the creditor the right to a specific action pursuing the thing pledged wherever it might be, pignus appears to be relatively old, but this does not imply that pignus also gave rise to a contractual action. There is no evidence that there ever existed a contractual action at Roman civil law, [38] but the praetor certainly gave one by his Edict no later than the first century B.C.[39] At the very least, the praetorian action is much more prominent than any presumed civil law action, and its wording is revealing: "If it appears that Aulus Agerius [the plaintiff] delivered to Numerius Negidius [the defendant] the thing which is the object of this action, as a pledge because of money that was owing; and that money has been paid, or satisfaction made on that account, or it was due to Numerius Negidius that payment was not made, and that thing has not been returned to Aulus Agerius, whatever the matter in issue will come to . . ." and so on. The so-called *iudicium con-*

trarium was also available to the creditor (D.13.7.9.pr.; 13.6.16.1), but there is no doubt that the primary, and perhaps at one stage the sole, contractual action lay to the debtor against the creditor. The main thrust of introducing the contract was thus the protection of the debtor. The real security of pignus could be made without delivery, but as the wording of the action indicates, there was a contract only if the pledge had been delivered to the creditor, and the contract gave rise to an action only when the debtor had repaid the loan or made satisfaction. Thus, in at least the great majority of cases, there could have been no physical obstacle to a stipulation. Even if delivery was not by the debtor personally but by someone in the power of the debtor, such as a son or slave, to the creditor or delivery was made to someone in the creditor's power, a legally binding stipulation could have been taken. The *actio quod iussu*, which would (for our purposes) make a head of household liable for a stipulatio made on account of his transaction by one of his dependants, is unlikely to be much later than contractual pignus.[40] And since the transaction is commercial, moral obstacles to taking a stipulation of the kind already mentioned would not here have existed. Tentatively, I would suggest a possible reason for the introduction within the tradition of Roman contract law. It rests on the premise that in the normal case, from the inside point of view, however unscrupulous or disreputable a lender might be, it is he who is doing the borrower a favor. The emphasis is on the fact that the borrower needs the cash, and the lender has it and is willing to lend. The borrower will not always be able to insist easily on taking a stipulation from the lender for the return of the thing after payment. The very request for a formal promise to do one's obvious moral duty implies distrust. Although it might be objected that an honest lender would have no qualms about giving a stipulation, the legal action is not needed for transactions that go well but for those that go wrong, and it is obviously aimed primarily at the dishonest creditor.[41]

But suppose one did not find an approach of this kind to be

plausible, insisting instead that an explanation had to be sought in economic or social needs for the emergence of the contract of pignus? That explanation would not be found. It is difficult to envisage much economic or social pressure for the new contractual action even when no stipulation was taken. Thus, when the repaid creditor failed or refused to return the thing pledged, the former debtor would have the ordinary action available to an owner claiming his property, which by this date would be the *vindicatio*. Where the creditor's behavior was theftuous, the debtor would have in addition the action on theft, the *actio furti*, for a penalty. Even if one assumes that from the beginning, as certainly later, the *formula* was also intended to give the action where the creditor returned the pledge in a damaged condition— and given the wording the assumption seems implausible—then the debtor already had a right of action under the *lex Aquilia*, where it was the creditor or someone in his power who did the damage, negligently or maliciously. The one situation previously unprovided for but now covered by the contractual action (and within straightforward interpretation of the wording) is where the creditor failed to return the pledge because it had been stolen from him in circumstances in which he had been negligent. For much the same reasons, there can have been little economic need for the contract of *commodatum*, or, as we have seen, of *depositum*.

It would not be surprising—though there is no positive evidence—if the praetorian actions on deposit, loan for use, and pledge are historically linked. The action of the Twelve Tables on deposit was the result of moral outrage, and much later, the Edict moderated the damages in most cases to simple restitution. Loan for use was seen not to be dissimilar; hence, likewise, a contractual action was given where property in the hands of one person as a result of agreement was not duly returned to the owner; and pignus (which may or may not be older than commodatum) was seen as another example.

We have no real indications of how or when or to what end the literal contract arose, and hence no argument can be drawn from it for or against any theory of the growth of Roman contract law. It was in existence by around the beginning of the first century B.C. (Cicero, *De officiis* 3.58) but may well be much older. In classical law it arose when a Roman head of family marked in his account books that a debt had been paid when it had not, then made an entry to the effect that a loan had been made when it had not.[42] It was thus not an originating contract but a method of transforming one kind of obligation into another. Whether that was also the case when the literal contract first came into being, and whether in the beginning the writing had to be in the formal account books is not clear.[43] The action was the *actio certae pecuniae* and therefore had to be for a fixed amount for money. The literal contract was flourishing in A.D. 70 when Pompeii was destroyed by the eruption of Vesuvius, but it had apparently disappeared from use by the end of the classical period.

Only one standard Roman contract, *societas* (partnership), remains to be dealt with, and its origins and growth are unique. The oldest Roman partnership, *ercto non cito*, is very old and came into being when a head of family died and his estate went to his *sui heredes* (G.3.154a), that is persons who were subject to his paternal power and on his death came to be free of any power. They were immediately partners in the inheritance and remained so until the inheritance was divided. Since in early Rome, persons in the power of another owned no property, the *sui heredes* had nothing until the inheritance came their way: hence *ercto non cito* is a partnership of all the property of the partners. This is not a contractual partnership, but later, persons who wished to set up such a partnership were allowed to do so by means of a *legis actio*, the archaic form of process, before the praetor (G.3.154b). Eventually the praetor gave an action on a consensual contract of partnership, perhaps around the time when he created the consensual contracts of sale and hire. But this consensual contract of partnership was modeled on the old *ercto non cito:* significantly, the praetor set out in his Edict only one *formula*, a model form of action, and that was for a partnership of all of the assets of the partners. Hence, the primary type of consensual partnership was not a commercial arrangement between merchants—they would want a much more restricted partnership—but between close relatives and friends, probably wishing to engage in a communal agricultural enterprise.[44] Rome had long been commercially active, a business partnership would clearly have been economically useful, but because of legal history and legal tradition the primary instance of consensual partnership was not mercantile. Whether from the outset, as certainly later, there could also be partnerships of a restricted kind cannot be determined.

This origin of partnership in succession and not in business accounts for a significant peculiarity in consensual partnership. An heir was liable for the debts of the deceased, even if they exceeded the assets. Co-heirs would be liable for debts in the same proportion as they inherited. Hence, the jurist Quintus Mucius Scaevola (killed in 82 B.C.) claimed that it was contrary to the nature of partnership that it be so set up that one partner was to take a greater share of any eventual profit than he would take of any eventual loss (G.3.149). Mucius' view is expressly based on the nature of partnership as he sees it, not on fairness. Though Servius Sulpicius broke away from this approach and successfully argued that such a partnership, and even one where one partner was entitled to share in the profit but not in any loss, was valid because that could be a fair arrangement if his services were valuable, yet Sabinus and Ulpian held that such an arrangement was valid only if in fact it was fair.[45] This is the sole instance in classical Roman law where a voluntary contractual arrangement entered into without error, coercion, or fraud was valid only if there was an equivalence of contribution and reward.[46] It owes its existence entirely to the internal logic of the legal tradition, and not at all to economic, social, or political pressures. It is this same legal logic and the piecemeal development of Roman contracts, and not societal forces, that prevented the necessity for equivalence from spreading to the other bilateral contracts or from being extinguished for partnership.

The force of this internal legal logic is apparent in another failure to develop. The contracts of deposit, loan for use, and mandate grew up one by one, but once they were all in existence there was no reason for not subsuming deposit and loan for use under mandate, except that they were in fact thought of as separate institutions. It is no obstacle that deposit and commodatum required delivery of the thing for the creation of the contract. The practical effect of the law would be unchanged if these contracts were incorporated into mandate: so long as nothing had been done on a mandate either party was free to revoke or renounce unilaterally.[47] There might even be doubt at times, as Pomponius discovered, whether a particular arrangement was mandate or deposit (D.16.3.12–14).

But the force on legal development of the lawyers' ways of looking at problems is even clearer when we look at contracts that did not develop or developed only partially or late. To begin with, it is prima facie astonishing that the Romans never developed a written contract that would take its place by the side of stipulatio as a second contract defined by form, not by function. Such a contract would obviously have been very useful, above all for situations where the stipulatio would have been the obvious contract except that the parties could not easily be present together: these situations would include sales where warranties against eviction or latent defects were wanted. Again, a contract whose validity depended on the existence of writing would usually be easy to prove. In fact, other contracts, including stipulatio, were often reduced to writing partly in order to provide proof,[48] partly to ensure that the terms were not forgotten. Nor can the Romans have been unaware of the possibility or the usefulness of written contracts: they had been standard even in classical Athens.[49] And the jurist Gaius in the second century A.D. was well aware of the existence of Greek written contracts and of the contrast between them and the Roman literal contract (G.3.134). The absence of such a contract demands an explanation, and that cannot be either economic or social. The most plausible explanation, I suggest, is that originally stipulation was the only contract, at a time when writing was not widespread. The habit was so ingrained of looking at stipulatio as *the* contract that other contracts arose as exceptions to or derogations from it only when stipulatio was obviously inappropriate. The idea of creating a new type of contract defined by form which could be used in all situations where stipulatio could be used and in other situations where it could not just did not occur to the Roman lawyers.

Likewise, it is equally astonishing that no contract of barter developed until the Empire at the earliest. Until the introduction of coined money around 275 B.C.,[50] a barter-type situation must have been the most common type of commercial transaction. Even afterwards, barter would be a frequent transaction. Yet barter, *permutatio,* as a legal institution is centuries later than the contract of sale, and it was never fully accepted into the Roman system of contracts.[51] As a contract it was very unsatisfactory: it required for its formation delivery by one party, and an action for nonperformance lay only for the value of the delivered goods. Contrast this with the contract of sale, which required only the agreement of the parties, and where the action lay for a sum of money equal to what the defendant ought to give or do in accordance with good faith. Nor can one say that the all-purpose stipulatio made a contract of barter unnecessary, since the stipulatio required an oral question and answer, and hence required the contracting parties to be face-to-face. The only way two merchants in different places could make an agreement for a barter situation was for one of them to send to the other, often at considerable expense and inconvenience, a dependent member of his family, such as a son or a slave, to take delivery or engage in mutual stipulationes. To say that Roman merchants did not engage much in barter is to forget that the introduction of coined money into Rome is relatively late, and to say that the Roman merchants would not find the law relating to barter inconvenient is to render inexplicable the introduction of such a splendid contract as sale. But the individual Roman contracts emerged— certainly because of societal needs—at a pace and with characteristics dictated by legal reasoning. Nothing illustrates this more clearly than a dispute between the Sabinian and the Proculian schools of jurists as to whether the price in a contract of sale could consist of a thing other than coined money (G.3.141; J.3.23.1; D.19.4.1.pr.). The Sabinians, who claimed that it could, relied on a text of Homer for the proposition that barter is the oldest form of sale:[52] the Proculians, who prevailed, claimed that the Sabinians had mistranslated and also argued that on that basis one could not determine what was the thing sold and what was the thing bought. At the root of the dispute is the serious business of extending satisfactory legal rules to barter. But the Sabinians, who were conscious of the economic realities, were bound by the rules of the legal game and could not come out and argue for more desirable rules for barter: the most they could do was argue that barter was included within the concept of sale. At no point, moreover, could they argue for legal change on social or economic grounds. The Proculians, who may or may not have been blind to the economic realities, also produced arguments of a purely legal nature for their successful position.[53] Law is being treated as if it were an end in itself. This indicates the existence of legal blindness. Apart from instances where it was morally impossible to demand a stipulation, the only derogations from stipulatio which were allowed to create a contract were those that involved an obligation to pay money: sale and the residual category of hire. It took even sale a very long time to break loose from the shackles of stipulatio.

Daube, as in the case of mutuum, feels that an explanation is needed for the failure to recognize a consensual contract of barter as early as sale, and even much later. And he finds that this "phenomenon is the result of the essentially intimate nature of moneyless barter as opposed to the distant aura in money-geared sale. Even at present, as a rule, an arrangement to swap records, cameras, houses (or partners) is more private and less law-oriented than one to transfer any of these possessions for money." And he offers a similar explanation for the failure to develop a contract akin to hire except in that neither of the prestations was in money.[54] Now there is, I believe, undoubtedly much truth in the argument, but the problem of the non-appearance of these contracts is perhaps greater than Daube suggests. First, intimate contracts not involving money pre-stations, such as deposit and loan for use, were recognized, provided always that they were gratuitous. Secondly, barter between merchants would be much less intimate than the mod-ern examples Daube suggests, especially in the days before coined money. For the absence of these transactions from the list of contracts one must add to the fact of no prestation in money the legal tradition that recognized only the stipulatio as a con-tract except when sufficient pressure arose in a very specific type of situation for the acceptance of a derogation from the stipulatio. Except when money was involved, that pressure was greater where the obligation was seen to be obviously friendly, involving trust, hence gratuitous.

Perhaps as early as the first century A.D., the Roman jurists began to devise remedies to plug gaps in the contractual system (D.19.5); the remedy for barter seems to have been one of them. The jurist Paul in the second or third century A.D. eventually stated that an action would be given on any agreement of the following types provided the plaintiff had performed his side of the bargain: "I give to you in order that you give, I give in order that you do, I do in order that you give, I do in order that you do" (D.19.5.5.pr.). Thereafter, any agreement containing bilateral obligations which was followed by performance by one party gave rise to an action. It is sometimes said that this is a step towards a general theory of contract. This seems incorrect. Each individual type of contract remained, each with its own major quirks. There was still no general contract law.

Finally, we should return to the oldest contract, stipulatio, which despite its long history never developed to its proper extent for reasons to be associated with the legal tradition. It is only to be expected that a very early contract is rigid, that the promisor is bound by what he says, and that the reason for his promise, even error, fraud or intimidation, is irrelevant. But once it came to be accepted, especially for the consensual contracts, that the obligations could be based on good faith, then only lawyerly conservatism and tradition would keep stipulatio a contract of strict law. There are societal advantages for the law taking good faith into account for contracts, and there is no social class of cheats. But no remedy was provided with regard to stipulatio for extortion or fraud until the first century B.C. Remedies for extortion were introduced by a praetor Octavius around 80 B.C. and for fraud by Aquillius Gallus apparently in 66 B.C.[55] What concerns us are the special defenses, *exceptiones*, of extortion or fraud, which could be raised when an action was brought on a stipulatio. The point of an exceptio is precisely that the defendant is not denying the validity of the plaintiff's case. He is merely claiming that there is another fact that ought to be taken into account. In other words, extortion or fraud did not invalidate a stipulatio. It remained valid but its effects could be negatived by the use of the defense. Stipulatio always remained at this primitive level. Nor should it be thought that the distinction between invalidity and blocking by an exceptio is insignificant: if the defendant failed to plead the exceptio expressly at the appropriate time, he could not plead it later and would lose his case. No explanation for retaining a stipulation as valid but rendering it ineffective is satisfactory other than that of lawyers' ideas of what is appropriate in law.

The main thrust of this part of the chapter has been that it was Roman legal thinking, based on a tradition rooted in stipulatio as the original contract, that above all dictated the origins and nature of Roman contracts. Though *societas* does not develop as a derogation from stipulatio, the mature contract, in its origins and nature, and also in a unique and important rule, equally demonstrates the enormous role of the legal tradition in legal evolution. None of this, of course, excludes an input by economic forces or by the politics of power. But this input of forces outside the legal tradition did not have a commensurate outcome. Nothing illustrates this more clearly than the relatively early actionability of contracts of depositum, commodatum, and pignus on the one hand, and the late appearance and continuing unsatisfactory state of *permutatio* on the other. It is not just that the first three, individually and collectively, are of much lesser commercial importance than barter; it is also that they were scarcely needed in view of existing actions in property and delict, whereas attempts to engage with legal protection in barter at a distance were fraught with inconvenience and expense. And it is surely hard to believe that the Roman merchants and others who engaged in barter had less political clout than the persons who deposited their property or lent it or used it as security for a loan.

The questions must be put whether one can generalize the enormous impact of the legal tradition on the evolution of the Roman law of contract or whether one should regard it as an exception in legal development. The second question can be dismissed out of hand, for two very obvious reasons. First, the development we have been looking at extended over more than a millenium, even though we concentrated only on the first five hundred years. Exceptional circumstances producing exceptional results are quite unlikely to last so long. Second, this is no unimportant, tiny branch of the law in a barren system, but the whole of contract law in the most imaginative secular legal system, a system which still has an impact almost fifteen hundred years after its demise with Justinian. All this is without taking into account the fact that similar patterns of development are to be found in many other circumstances.

But how far can one generalize? At this stage we should note three important reservations. First, we have been concerned with a mature legal system. How law develops in a system of customary law is the subject of the next chapter. Secondly, we have been looking at one system, remarkable for its self-reliance. Borrowings from other legal systems, even a careful appraisal of other peoples' legal rules, is remarkably limited at Rome. Scholars do disagree on the impact of foreign law, especially of Greek and Semitic law, in Rome,[56] but no one doubts that the input of the Romans themselves was exceptionally great. Hence it might be suggested that the Roman experience is unique, and that elsewhere the impact of the legal tradition is less pronounced. On the contrary, purely on a priori grounds—but the notion must be tested—one would expect that the more home-grown the product, the less would be the impact of the legal tradition of the legal elite. The reason is obvious. Speaking generally, only the legal elite of a society know anything about foreign law: only they are in a position to organize a borrowing. Thirdly, the Romans did not make much use of statute law, though it was available to them. Statute law is now the main vehicle of fundamental legal change. Perhaps it may be suggested that what happened at Rome has few lessons for the analysis of modern legal change. And I would be the first to concede that the sources of law, available and made use of, have an enormous impact on legal change.[57]

Paternity Suits

In any attempt to measure the force of reservations two and three above, one point must always be borne in mind, namely that, with a blinkered view, almost every legal development can be explained, wrongly but understandably, on purely societal terms. It is unlikely that a society will accept an entirely inappropriate legal rule; and scholarly skill can always point to conditions in a society favoring the particular change, while downplaying conditions hostile to the change. To uncover the truth we often, therefore, have no choice but to consider legal rules comparatively as well as sociologically. An example will make this plain, while also casting light on legal borrowing and telling us something about legal change in modern conditions when statute law is so prominent.

One would expect, if one believed in a close relationship between law and society, that legal rules that affected the sexes differently would tell us much about the position of women in society. One would expect that that position would be affected by societal circumstances—economic, such as whether the society was slave, feudal, developing capitalist, capitalist, or post-capitalist; religious, such as whether the society was Muslim, Hindu, or Christian—and hence that these circumstances would be reflected in the law. And no one will deny that there is and must be some correlation. The problem is to find the correlation. For instance, there is no doubt but that the social and economic position of the unmarried mother is a sad one in most societies. How sad will depend in part on general societal conditions and attitudes: on the value placed on female chastity, on religious and moral beliefs, on the work available for women, on family structures and their strength, on male domination. But the burden on the mother is infinitely greater if she must alone bear the economic cost, if she cannot bring a paternity suit against the supposed father for partial maintenance of the child. Here we should expect to see societal circumstances reflected in the law. And countries do differ in this regard. Around 1870, the general position was as follows: These legal jurisdictions allowed a paternity suit: England, Sweden, Norway, Denmark, Austria, Bavaria, Prussia, Spain, Scotland, Hungary, Saxony, Würtenburg, Bern, Zurich, Glaris, Freiburg, Brazil, Peru, Chile, Guatemala, El Salvador, Honduras, Lower Canada, and many of the U.S. states. These denied paternity suits: Sardinia, Naples, Italy, France, Belgium, Holland, Haiti, Hesse, Luxembourg, Geneva, Ticino, some German states on the Rhine, Russia, Greece, Neufchatel, Vaud, Serbia, Rumania, Monaco, Costa Rica, Bolivia, Uruguay, and Venezuela.[58] But what do those in one list have in common, which is absent from those in the other list? It can scarcely be a religion, whether Catholic or Protestant or otherwise, or the general state of economic development, or climate. Nor is it obviously a view of the sanctity of the family. In short, one cannot say that women's status or social attitudes toward women determined the law on this important point. The explanation of this difference is to be sought above all in the legal tradition, and primarily in the strong reliance on Napoleon's *Code Civil* of 1804 in the states that refused the suit. Hence is to be explained the appearance of the French-speaking Swiss cantons on that list, the German-oriented cantons on the other; Belgium, Holland, Rumania, Hesse, and Rhineland states on that list, other German states on the other. It might be thought that the allowing of such an action in Lower Canada and Louisiana spoke against this explanation. But the law of Lower Canada, so far as it was French-dominated, was based on earlier French law. And the law of Louisiana, here as often, was based on Spanish law, as the particular provisions of the *Digest* of 1808[59] and the *Code* of 1825[60] show. (It will be recalled that Spain took formal possession of Louisiana in 1769, that France retook possession on November 30, 1803, and that Louisiana was surrendered to the United States on December 20, 1803.)

None of the foregoing should be taken to imply that there was no input from the society. Thus, Louisiana, as one might expect, did not allow the action in favor of nonwhite children.[61] And, of course, particular reasons can be adduced for the change by revolutionary law and at the time of Napoleon to the famous rule of article 340: "La recherche de la paternité est interdite." To begin with, at that time, disputed paternity was very difficult to prove or disprove even within the standards of proof regarded as sufficient in a court action. Yet it must be stressed that often there would be enough evidence to show that the defendant in fact thought he was or could well be the father. So the difficulties of proof are not a sufficient reason for the total ban on paternity suits. There were also fears that such actions could lead to public scandals and the distress of the defendant's family. Of course, insofar as the latter point is a serious one, and the distress of the defendant's family deserves to be given more weight than the worries of the mother, most of the possible pain would have disappeared had the rule been that no paternity suit could be brought when the effect would be to make the child adulterine or the result of incest. Further, it is said that Napoleon, who supported article 340, was worried lest his soldiers have their minds taken off more important matters by having to respond to paternity suits.[62] But the origins of the rule go further back than Napoleon's concern. Cambacérès' unsuccessful second "projet" of 1795 contains a version of the rule, which reads: "La loi n'admet pas la recherche de la paternité non avouée."[63] Finally, and probably most importantly, the previous French law had come into disrepute. There was a maxim, *creditur virgini parturienti*, "a maiden giving birth is believed," which was enforced every time an unmarried woman of previous good reputation named someone as the father. Admittedly, the order was only interlocutory, and full proof had later to be established, but Bigot-Préameneu could insist that anyone could be the victim of unjustified attack and that "paternity suits were regarded as the bane of society."[64] The draftsmen of the *Code Civil*—Portalis, Tronchet, Bigot-Préameneu, and Maleville—set out their reasons in the *Discours préliminaire du premier projet de code civil:* "The law presuming nothing, and being unable to presume anything, for children born of a union that it does not admit, it is necessary that those children be recognized by the authors of their days in order that they may claim their rights. If it was otherwise, the honor of women, the peace of households, the fortune of citizens, would be continually at risk. New laws have provided for the evil and, in this regard, we keep the provisions of these laws."[65]

From the law on paternity suits—at least in countries other than France—we might be justified in reaching the conclusion that societal concerns were relevant for the law but only negatively. Some or even most societies might find either approach acceptable. The solution proposed by the legal tradition would be rejected by a society only if for other reasons it were found to be intolerable. The law here also indicates what was not apparent from Roman contract law, that even in the age of statute much of legal development is dictated by the legal tradition and not by the general makeup of the society or its ruling elite. Moreover, just as the Roman law of contract shows that economic realities impinged but little on legal change, so religion and morality, views on the family, and the status of women were not generally decisive on an issue important to all three.

The foregoing discussion, moreover, indicates the futility of trying to explain a society's legal rules by societal conditions, independently of the legal tradition, and the need for the use of comparative legal history. If we had nothing of a society but its law at a particular time, we could reconstruct relatively little of its values or circumstances except for the most obvious. We live in a world very different from that which seems to be implied in the rhetorical question of P. D. King: "[For] what testimony reflects more faithfully and fully than law the ideological assumptions of the society which produces it or, at least, of the governing circles of that society?"[66] What conclusions, after all, would we draw about French society on the eve of the French Revolution and a decade later from the law just discussed?[67]

Yet the creation or alteration of a legal rule, whether borrowed or not, has societal consequences except where the rule remains only "law in books" and is not also "law in action." There are also other means of social control which will affect the impact of a legal rule: the same rule can operate differently in different societies. Even taking these into account, it is striking how tolerant society is of law that is not peculiarly adapted to it and how enormous a role society allows the legal elite to play in shaping the law.

The Normative Fact of Law

Lawyers, indeed, come to treat law as fact—normative fact, of course, but still something existing in its own right. Faced with a legal problem, lawyers contemplate the societal facts of the issue and the normative facts of the law that have to be applied to them to come up with the answer. The societal facts and the normative facts may be equally hard to discover.

Law develops by lawyers thinking about the normative facts, whether in the abstract or in relation to hypothetical or actual societal facts. A course becomes set which is difficult to alter. In this part of the chapter we will look at a few short examples where past legal thinking boxed lawyers into a situation from which reasonable escape was impossible in the absence of drastic action, and where the result was both unwanted by the lawyers, who nevertheless, could see no appropriate way out, and also remote from the ways of thinking of the rest of society.[68]

A first example is taken from the Roman law of theft, which was treated primarily as a delict, a private wrong, rather than a crime. It was early settled that the necessary act for the commission of theft was wrongful handling (*contrectatio*), not asportation (as for instance in the English law of larceny), and that the action lay to the victim for a multiple, double or quadruple, of the value of what was stolen. The wrongful intent was probably—there is some dispute—an undifferentiated intention to make a gain: it certainly was not (again, as it is in English law) the intention to deprive the owner permanently. These normative facts were deeply embedded in the Roman jurists' brains. But taken together they gave rise to a problem with no straightforward legal answer; when the thief took, and wanted, only part of a whole. The wine in a barrel is *one* thing: if someone takes and wants only a cupful, he nonetheless has touched the whole of the wine. The relevant wrongful act is not the taking away; hence the object stolen cannot be restricted to what he actually removed. The relevant wrongful intention is not the permanent deprivation of the owner: hence again the fact that the thief did not want all of the wine cannot be used to limit the extent of his theft. The action is for a multiple of the value of the thing stolen, not of the owner's interest; hence the thief has to pay double the value of all of the wine. The result has savage and horrific implications.

The earliest case seems to be discussed in the late Republic. Someone removed a bushel out of a heap of wheat: the jurist Ofilius declared this to be theft of the whole heap.[69] Likewise, the same text tells us that removal of a small quantity from a cask of wine is theft of the whole cask. Two and a half centuries later, the problem was not resolved. Ulpian, in one particular situation, has a solution: if someone breaks open a chest which is too heavy for him to carry, he is not liable to an action for all of the contents but only for what he took, "because he could not take the whole" (D.47.2.21.8). Scarcely a convincing argument. Most revealing of all is another part of Ulpian's discussion of the problem:

> If anyone theftuously removed a *sextarius* of wheat from a whole shipload, has he committed theft of the whole shipload or only of the *sextarius?* The question is easier with regard to a full granary; and it is hard to say that the theft is of the whole. And what would one say if it were a cistern of wine? Or of water? And what would we say about him who drew off some wine from a ship of wine, and there are many ships into which wine is simply poured? Is he the thief of the whole cargo? And it is more likely[70] that we would say he is the thief not of the whole. (D.47.2.21.5)

The great Ulpian has no solution. He thinks the answer ought to be that the thief does not have to pay a multiple of the whole value. But within the framework of legal argument he does not know how to get there. Hence, his very weak answer: "It is more likely that we would say he is the thief not of the whole." The answers are hesitant; they tend only to disagree with the previously accepted answer but do not give a positive, possible solution, still less any reasons for one.[71]

It is worth stressing that one cannot find a neat sociological explanation for the jurists' attitudes. One cannot say either that the jurists were willing to take a stern attitude, or were basically uninterested in the problem, because the thief would usually be from the poorer and less influential strata of society, whereas the victim would be propertied and closer to the jurists in social standing. The fact is that many Roman thieves would be slaves, and the private law action would then lie against the owner (who could be very like the jurists in standing), who would have to pay the multiple of the value unless he surrended the slave.

A second example is chosen from the famous Rule against Perpetuities of English law, which was transported elsewhere, including America. The classic description of it is not statutory but derives from an academic writer, J. C. Gray: "No interest is good, unless it must vest, if at all, not later than 21 years after some life in being at the creation of the interest."[72] An interest is vested when there is an immediate fixed right of present or future enjoyment. The Rule is not to the effect that an interest must vest—because it is concerned with contingent interests—but only that if it does it will of necessity do so not later than twenty-one years after some life in being at the creation of the interest.

The Rule may be said to have grown out of medieval legal antagonism to attempts to keep land within a family in perpetuity. The main steps in the development of the modern Rule can be rapidly plotted.[73] Lord Nottingham settled in the *Duke of Norfolk's Case* (1681–85) that an interest that must vest, if it ever did, not later than expiration of a life in being was good.[74] The decision did not, however, settle the maximum period within which an interest had to vest if it were to be valid. In 1736, the case of *Stephens* v. *Stephens*[75] determined that a devise to the unborn child of a life in being on the attainment of twenty-one by the child was good. Thus, the maximum period within which the interest must vest, if at all, was extended. In 1805, by *Thelluson* v. *Woodford*[76] it was settled that any number of lives might be selected, who had no connection with the settled property, provided they were not so numerous as to make it impossible to determine the survivor. *Cadell* v. *Palmer*[77] confirmed this, and also determined that the "reasonable time" after the expiration of a life in being in which the interest must vest, if at all, was twenty-one years, and that this period need be connected with minorities. Thus was the modern Rule established by which subsequent generations lived. There have been variations by statute in various jurisdictions, but we need not consider these. What does matter for us is that by apparently reasonable steps in legal thinking a monstrosity was created which is far from the thinking of lay persons and which cannot be understood in its working by the majority of lawyers.[78]

A few examples will indicate the operation and difficulties of the Rule.[79] In each example, the use of the capital letter A, indicates a life in being.

(1) *"To the first child of A to marry."* Void. The child of A who is first to marry might not yet be a life in being, and he need not marry within twenty-one years of A's death.

(2) *"To the first child of A to attain twenty-one years."* Valid. A cannot procreate after his death, so the interest must vest, if at all, within twenty-one years of his death (plus the allowable period of gestation if the child is posthumous).

(3) *"When a house ceases to be maintained as a dwelling house."* Void. The house may be maintained as a dwelling house long after the termination of a life in being plus twenty-one years. The legal logic is remorseless. Only the possibility that the vesting might occur after the permitted period is taken into account. Reality is excluded. The gift remains void even if the dwelling house is in such disrepair that renovation is financially almost inconceivable or is in an area about to be turned over exclusively to industry. Likewise, "when the next human lands on the moon" makes the devise void even though a country has active plans to land another human on the moon within three years: the plan might be abandoned.

(4) *"To A for life, then on her death to any husband she may marry for his life, then on the death of the survivor to any of their children then living."* Void as to the gift to the children. A may marry a

husband who is not yet born, and he may survive her for more than twenty-one years.

(5) *"To A for life, then on her death to any husband she may marry for his life, and then to any children of A at twenty-one."* Valid. The bequest vests in interest when the children reach twenty-one, and this cannot be outside of the permitted period.

(6) *"To my widow, then, on her death, to be held in trust for my nephews when they reach twenty-one."* Valid if the testator has no parent living at the time of his death. His brothers and sisters are lives in being, so his nephews cannot attain twenty-one outside of the permitted period. Void if the testator has a parent living at the time of his death. The law takes no account here of physical, but only of legal, possibility or impossibility. The testator's mother may be a centenarian at the time of his death; still the law takes into account that she may later conceive and give birth. Her child then would not be a life in being, and his children would reach twenty-one after the extinction of the lives in being.

Leading authorities have opined: "The Rule against Perpetuities undoubtedly has produced many hard cases where some unskilled or unfortunate draftsman has inadvertently broken the Rule although no threat to the public interest can be shown to have existed."[80] It should be stressed that the Rule comes into operation no matter what the intention of the testator or settler was, and even though he firmly expected the interest to vest within a few years. The authors just quoted could also say of the operation of the Rule in America: "The fact is that there are many cases and some statutes in the United States that deserve only to be placed in a bottle on some laboratory shelf beside the twoheaded goat foetuses." They do, however, conclude "that on the whole, the Rule does more good than harm, though the policy considerations underlying it are much weaker than they were 300 or 100 years ago."[81]

There are certainly good arguments for believing some time limit on the vesting of future interests to be necessary. But the way the Rule developed within the legal tradition led to an impasse with no way out, except by means of a drastic statutory remedy. There have been many statutory modifications, not always satisfactory, to the Rule in various jurisdictions. For England, the Perpetuities and Accumulations Act of 1964 brought vital changes.

It should be noted that the persons whose intentions would not be given effect as a result of the Rule were not the poor: only the propertied make settlements or testaments.

A third and final example may be chosen from French law. The French *Code Civil* treats delicts and quasi-delicts in a remarkably small number of articles. Articles 1382 and 1383 make liability for damage caused to another rest squarely on fault, including negligence, and this has to be proved by the plaintiff; but article 1384 is less specific: "One is liable not only for the loss one causes by one's own act, but also for that which is caused by someone for whom one is responsible or for things that one has under one's guard."

The connection between articles 1383 and 1384, previous French law and legislative history all, however, indicate that one is liable also for things under one's guard also only for fault. That is likewise the logical interpretation of the wording of article 1384: one is liable for one's own act and for the act of persons for whom one is responsible. In the absence of any statement to the contrary, the two situations ought to be treated alike. If fault is required for the first, then also for the second. Certainly, at any rate, liability in the second cannot be greater than in the first. But one is liable for one's own act, for the act of persons for whom one is responsible, and for things under one's guard. The standard of liability for the third situation cannot be different from the standard of liability in the first two.

Thus, liability for things under one's guard should be only for fault of the defendant which could be shown by the plaintiff, and this was the approach at first taken by the courts.[82] But this could not be entirely satisfactory, given the frequency of industrial injuries where the defendant's fault often could not be established. So other solutions were sought, for instance on the basis of contract. Another approach was to make the guardian of the object liable if the object could be shown to be defective.[83] But, especially after a violent explosion, a defect in the object often could not be proved, so a further judicial step was taken. If an object caused damage, there was a presumption of fault on the part of the person who had the object under his guard, and this presumption could be rebutted only by the proof of *cas fortuit, force majeure,* or a *cause étrangère* that cannot be imputed to him.[84] Thus, to avoid liability it would not be enough for the defendant to show he was not at fault, and for liability to attach it was not necessary that the object have an inherent defect capable of causing the damage.[85]

It is at this stage that matters get out of hand because of the impact of legal reasoning, with effects contrary to the common sense of the layman, and drastic intervention, obviously by statute, is necessary to set things right.

Two problems stand out. First, it is a principle of French law that one cannot draw a distinction where the law does not draw one; and article 1384 does not draw a distinction between a moving object and a stationary one. Hence, for example, if damage is caused by an automobile in motion, the person who has it under his guard is automatically liable under 1384 even if there was no defect in the automobile, unless the damage was caused by *cas fortuit, force majeure,* or an external cause that cannot be imputed to him. Liability is on account of the object, not the driver's behavior. Although under article 1382 a person is liable for his own acts only if he is at fault, the driver of a car is liable under 1384 whether he was negligent or not and whether or not there was any defect in the car.[86] A decision of this kind prompted the comment of the distinguished jurist, George Ripert: "One would have to imagine a collision between two individuals practicing total nudity before there could be scope for the application of Art. 1382! Even then one might well find a jurist who would claim that the body is only an object under the guard of the will, and that consequently one must apply article 1384 to the damage due to the corporeal act of the man."[87] The issue for us, of course, is not whether a system of absolute liability or a system of no liability without fault is preferable. It is rather the intolerable conflict between articles 1382 and 1384 brought about by the application of legal reasoning as a consequence of a morally justifiable, deliberate misinterpretation of article 1384, and the consequent remoteness of legal debate from reality. Incidentally, physical contact between the object and the injured thing or person is not necessary. Hence, it is perhaps not surprising that in a recent case where a plaintiff skier fell and was injured either because of being touched, or because of being surprised and scared, by the defendant skier passing at high speed, the court held the defendant liable whether he physically touched her or not. The court held that whether the plaintiff's fall was caused by the sight of the skier or his skis, they formed a unit, and, since the skier's movement depended on his skis, that the skis were the instrument of injury. Again, of course, since liability was under article 1384, fault on the part of the defendant was not needed to make him liable.[88]

This leads right into the second issue. The approach taken by the courts in interpreting article 1384 apparently took liability out of the realm of fault[89] to base it squarely on causation. When injury was caused by an object, its guardian was liable unless the damage resulted from *cas fortuit, force majeure,* or an external cause which was not to be imputed to the guardian. But an object can cause injury whether it is in motion or not, and two objects (or an object and a person) are involved in any injury. Under this principle, if both are injured, each is the cause of the injury to the other. If I am riding my bicycle and almost collide with a Cadillac, each of us swerving so as to avoid hitting the other, but I strike the curb and bend my front wheel, whereas the Cadillac sails over a cliff, the guardian of the Cadillac or his heirs can be sued for the damage to my bicycle wheel, whereas I can be sued for the damage to the Cadillac. This liability can be excluded only if one object can be regarded as the purely passive cause. Thus, if a truck is parked at the side of the highway with its regulation lights on, and in the middle of the night, it is struck by a moving car, then if the guardian of the truck cannot prove that at the moment of collision his lights were still on, he will be liable to the guardian of the car for the damage to the car. Such a truck is not in a normal situation; hence it is not a passive object with regard to causation. In an actual case, a policeman verified that forty minutes beforehand the truck lights were on. That proved nothing for the moment of the collision, and the burden of proof was on the guardian of the truck to show that the cause of the accident was due to external force. The court treated the cause of the accident as unknown.[90]

The law is even more complex because it does bring in the notions of contributory negligence and of degrees of fault, but we need go no further. This is no small, trivial part of the law, but the core of French tort law. There have been recent statutory modifications. The striking fact for us is that they have been so few and so late. Lawyers habitually are very accepting of the state of the law. To an outsider I think it would seem perverse that in 1930, arguing in one of the cases just discussed, the procureur général could claim in the context of article 1384: "Every time one speaks with a foreign jurist, every time one discusses with him the scope of some article of our civil code, especially in the title 'On Obligations,' he never fails to express the profound admiration he has for texts which contain formulations so supple and so precise at the same time, so wide and comprehensive that, formulated in the time of horse-drawn carriages, they apply equally well to the automobile and even to the aeroplane."[91]

A general conclusion might be set at the end of this, and of every succeeding, chapter. Lawmakers are persons, with the limitations of human beings, steeped in their trade. Law produced through them or by them does not correspond to any "Spirit of the People" or "Spirit of the Ruling Class." Lawmakers have defects of imagination and restrictions of knowledge. They are part of society and share in the general culture and interests of society. But they develop a specialized attitude to law, arising out of the tradition in which they work. There is a lawyer's way to approach a problem. This mode of thinking inoculates them from too much concern with the demands of the society. Lawmaking becomes an art form that can be understood only by its practitioners. And this way of thinking, communicated to the other members of the society and the ruling class, leads non-lawyers to leave much of law reform to the lawmakers and generally to acquiesce in the results.[92]

II

Customary Law

Customary Law in Western Europe

A proper understanding of the nature of customary law—a source of law that has not yet been much discussed in this book—is important for Western legal historians. From post-Roman times to the beginning of the modern legal age in the eighteenth century, the two main elements in European law were Roman law and legal custom, the learned law and the other. In large measure, the main task of lawyers of that long stretch of time was the unification or harmonization of the two strands of Roman law and custom. Naturally, even before, customary law was important: in Rome before the Twelve Tables no doubt, and among the Germanic tribes before the codes beginning in the fifth century. But evidence for these days is slight, so the stress in this chapter will be on explaining the nature of customary law as it appears from, say, the eleventh century onwards.[1] Customary law is not all of one piece. It operates, for example, among wandering small groups, temporarily settled tribes, rather small permanent communities, and so on right into economically developed modern Western societies where there is also much statute law. The last type will be discussed in Chapter 4.

Customary law, of course, most flourishes in circumstances where law is likely to be least theoretical. Yet there must be theoretical underpinnings for the nature of any source of law, even if these underpinnings are always implicit and never expressed. For custom to be regarded as law in Western private law, more must be and is required than simple usage, even if the usage is general and has long been frequent. The issue, of course, is that one cannot simply equate an "ought" and an "is." The fact that people so behave does not indicate that they should so behave, and be subject to some sanction if they do not. What is it, above mere behavior, that makes the behavior normative? The main problem for any theory or understanding of customary law seems to be the determination of this additional factor. The Roman sources clearly imply that some additional factor is needed, even if the nature of this factor is not apparent. Thus: *Epitome Ulpiani*, 4. "Custom is the tacit consent of the people, deeply rooted through long usage." Here the additional factor is expressed by the otherwise tautological 'tacit consent' or 'tacit agreement' (*tacitus consensus*). But to what has tacit consent been given? Certainly it is not to the long usage itself: the tacit consent is rooted in the long usage. J.1.1.9. "Unwritten law is that which usage has approved. For long-practiced customs, endorsed by the consent of the users, take on the appearance of statute." This time the additional factor is expressed by "endorsed by the consent of the users" (*consensu utentium comprobati*). The vagueness of Ulpian has not been dissipated.

D.1.3.32.1 (Julian Digest 84). Deeply rooted custom is observed as a statute, not undeservedly; and this is what is called law established by usage. For since statutes themselves bind us for no other reason than because they have been accepted by the judgment of the people, then deservedly those things which the people have approved without writing will bind all. For what does it matter that the people declare its wish by vote or by positive acts and conduct?

Therefore, it is very rightly accepted that laws are abrogated not only by the vote of him who proposes law, but also through desuetude, by the tacit consent of all.

We need not discuss here the accuracy of Julian's account of the people's role in statute-making, or of custom bringing about the desuetude of statute. This time the nature of the additional factor seems to be clearer: for Julian it appears to be that the custom is law because the people accept it as law.[2]

For a long time after Justinian there seems to have been little advance in coming to grips with the issue,[3] but the idea of *opinio necessitatis*, which may by implication have its roots in the text of Julian, did eventually appear[4] and, despite some opposition, still appears to be dominant. The idea of opinio necessitatis is precisely that the persons involved purposely follow a certain rule because they believe that it is a rule of law. The idea has been explained by modern theorists like K. Larenz:

One can say the practice must be the expression of an "intention of legal validity" of the community or of a "general conviction of law," provided only that one is clear that this "intention of legal validity" or the "general conviction of law" is not solely a *"psychological fact,"* but the *"sense of fulfilling a norm"* (of a legally commanded behavior) developing or dwelling in the individual acts of conduct according to the judgment of those sharing the same law.[5]

On this view then, custom becomes law when it is known to be law, is accepted as law and practiced as law by the persons who share the same law. But suppose that, once the custom is known to be law and is accepted as law, the practice changes. Does the old law cease to be law, and the new practice come to be law? If this does happen, at what moment does it happen? And what is the machinery for change?

There are two different problem situations. First, the past custom is remembered. Secondly, the past custom is forgotten.

In the first situation, which is the one that is really important both in theory and in real life, it must be the case that the law cannot be changed by a contrary practice. So long as the past custom is remembered as being law, there can be no point on the continuum at which the new practice is used in consciousness that it is law. The outmoded practice must cease to be law before a different law can begin to emerge from customary usage; and within the theory there is no mechanism for deleting law that no longer commands approval.

One might try to get around this difficulty by postulating a doctrine of desuetude inherent in customary law: when a practice which has become blessed as law ceases to be followed or to be regarded as law, then, it may be claimed, it ceases to be law. At that stage, but not before, the road becomes clear, it might be suggested, for the creation of new customary law. The performance of the new custom before the old customary legal rule became obsolete is a factor in making the old legal rule obsolete, but not (always following the doctrine of opinio necessitatis) in creating a new legal rule because the new practice was not followed in "the general conviction of law." So at the moment of desuetude, there is no law on the point at all. But against this arises here in a particularly sharp form the objection raised by Friedrich von Savigny against opinio necessitatis within the framework usually attributed to custom.[6] Custom should not rest on error, a point expressly made in the Roman sources.[7] But then, he says, there is a contradiction without solution. For the rule of law should arise first through the custom, but at the time of the first behavior the law was of course not in existence. But this first relevant behavior should be accompanied by the opinio necessitatis. Consequently the first behavior rested on an error and should not be counted for the creation of the customary law. But this also applies to the second act of behavior, which now becomes the first, and so on to all subsequent acts.

On this basis, under the received doctrine of opinio necessitatis and custom, it is logically impossible for customary behavior to create law. A fortiori, when the new customary behavior was being adopted when there already existed a different rule of customary law, any belief that the new behavior was conform to law was clearly grounded on error. If custom cannot create a legal rule, even less can it both create and substitute a new legal rule for an established rule that it abolishes.

In fact, if opinio necessitatis is at the root of customary law, it is very difficult to admit the possibility of desuetude of a customary legal rule, provided always that the legal rule is remembered. Customary law is, we are told, a "general conviction of law"; hence it corresponds to what people generally do, and they do it because it is the law. To act contrary to this would be a deviant act and unacceptable and contrary to law.[8] The point, it should be remembered, is not that customary behavior does not change: it is rather that, under the doctrine of opinio necessitatis, where a rule of customary law exists and is remembered, it cannot become obsolete by desuetude: contrary acting which is known to be contrary to the rule cannot affect it.

There is a further and more important logical difficulty in admitting the possibility of desuetude of customary law under a theory of opinio necessitatis. A legal rule can fall into desuetude only if it has been replaced by another legal rule, even if this later rule is only to the effect that the first rule no longer applies. But by the theory of opinio necessitatis, the new rule can come into existence only after it is established that the old known rule is extinct, since otherwise there could be no general conviction that the new behavior corresponds to the law. There is thus no scope for desuetude.

In the second situation also, where the past custom is forgotten, the law is not being changed by a contrary practice. If customary law is completely forgotten, then for all intents and purposes it does not exist and has not existed. There is not even any need to bring in here a theory of obsolescence. What would be involved is the creation of law where none existed before. Also the total forgetting of the customary law can happen only in particular circumstances.[9] Either the past behavior occurred very seldom in practice, in which case one must doubt whether it had ever become law as a result of common consciousness that it was law. Or the people had in this regard adopted a very different lifestyle—perhaps as a result of migration—in which case it should be argued that the new practice is law not because new law has replaced old law but because law has been created for circumstances where no law existed before. In any event, where a rule or supposed rule of customary law has been completely forgotten, one cannot admit that a subsequent contrary practice has, as law, replaced previously existing customary law.

Thus, the doctrine of opinio necessitatis excludes the possibility of changing customary law by subsequent practice, especially in the situation where the customary law is remembered. If one wishes to hold, as I believe theorists would wish to hold, that customary law should be in correspondence with what people do, then one would want any theory to countenance the possibility of changing the law by contrary practice. Opinio necessitatis must then on this basis be dismissed.

Savigny, despite his powerful argument against opinio necessitatis within the framework usually attributed to customary law, retains the notion. His solution rests on his general view of law as the "spirit of the people." Law does not arise from individual acts of behavior but from common consciousness. Thus, individual acts of behavior are not the cause of creation of customary law, but are the appearances or indications of a preexisting common conviction of law.[10] Hence, the opinio necessitatis exists before the first relevant act of behavior, which therefore does not rest on an error of law.[11] Opinio necessitatis is thus saved but only for a very different doctrine of the nature of customary law. The validity of Savigny's view of custom and opinio necessitatis depends on the plausibility of his general theory of law, which is today universally rejected, I think, by legal philosophers.[12] Hence it will not be further discussed here.

Thus, if we wish to retain as an element in customary law the power to change when practices change—and even perhaps if we wish a power in customary behavior to create law—we must abandon opinio necessitatis. A further conclusive objection against the theory will emerge implicitly from the following pages, namely that opinio necessitatis just cannot explain what actually happens in practice. A different theory, which may prove to be more acceptable, is suggested to me by the work of John Austin. According to him, customary laws considered as rules of positive morality arise from the consent of the governed; but considered as moral rules turned into positive laws customary laws are established by the state, either directly by statute, or circuitously when the customs are adopted by its tribunals.[13] Thus, customary behavior does not make law; law is made by legislation or by judicial decision. Custom becomes law only when it is the subject of statute or judicial decision.

Before we consider the value of this, we should first recognize that the proposition is not necessarily or obviously correct except to someone who, like Austin, holds that law is the command of a sovereign. Statute is law even before it is enforced by a decision of a court.[14] Hence, if other sources of law, such as custom, exist in possibility, then that law, too, may in possibility exist without benefit of a court decision. It may well be argued that "it is precisely the binding force of custom which challenges [Austin's] initial assumption itself," and that "he failed to explain satisfactorily why the body of rules which he classifies as 'positive morality' . . . lacked the true character of law."[15]

A second point that may be made is that societies that do not regard judicial decisions, even a consistent line of them, as binding precedents—that is, as law—may nonetheless treat decisions establishing a custom as binding. On this basis one might claim: judicial precedent is not law; custom is law. When a court finds that a custom exists, the decision in itself is not binding, but the preexisting custom which already is law has as a matter of fact been established; hence the decision (which is not law) expresses the law.

These two points have, or may have, great weight against Austin, but there are other factors which seem to lend support to his position.

In the first place, customary law very often does not grow from a "general conviction of law." In this case, legal decisions play a fundamental role in determining what is the rule of customary law. Thus, it is a standard complaint of those living under customary law who wish to reduce it to writing that the law is difficult to find, or know, or remember. Thus, to give a few examples, the famous Philippe de Beaumanoir (d. 1296) gives among the reasons for his *Coutumes de Beauvaisis:* "It is my opinion and of others also that all customs that are now used be written down and recorded so that they be maintained without change from now on, because through memories that are liable to fade and human life that is short what is not written is soon forgotten" (Prologue, sec. 71). In his *Conseil* (ca. 1260), which concerns the customs of Vermondais, Pierre de Fontaines claims that the old customs are much destroyed and almost all are defective, partly because of judges who prefer their own wishes to using the customs, partly because of those who are more attached to their own opinions than to the acts of earlier generations, and almost entirely because the rich despoiled the poor and now the poor despoil the rich. The country, he says, is almost without custom (chap. 1, sec. 3).

At the beginning of this century J. A. Brutails, in his celebrated work on the custom of Andorra, also brought out the difficulty of knowing customary law. He stresses that in a small place the number of lawsuits is limited, and in the absence of any methodical collection of decisions, the law in the cases fluctuates. He points out that even on contemporary and important matters there is at times a disconcerting incertitude. For instance, he asked prominent people, magistrates, former magistrates, and judges what were the rights of the widow over the property of her husband; and he received five different answers.[16] Indeed, he claimed often to have heard that Andorra had no custom, but Andorra seemed to him no different from other customary systems. Despite the numerous and significant gaps in the law it was not certain whether they were to be filled first by looking at Roman, canon, or Catalan law. The common view was the first, but he sought to demonstrate that in fact it was Catalan law that had usually prevailed.[17] It seems to me that Andorran legal sentiment now favors Roman law though in practice Catalan law may prevail.

King Charles VII of France's *Ordonnance de Montil-les-Tours*, dated April 1453, records that "it often happens that in one single region, the parties rely on contrary customs, and sometimes the customs are silent and vary at will, from which great hardships and loss affect our subjects" (art. 125).

In such situations, in the absence of official redactions of the customs which then hold sway as statute, court decisions embody the rules. As Philippe de Beaumanoir says for his unofficial redaction, "We intend to confirm a great part of this book by the judgments that have been made in our time in the said county of Clermont" (Prologue, sec. 6). Well worth quoting are the words of the Maître Echevin in the preface to the official redaction of the customs of Metz in 1613, after the work had supposedly been under active preparation since 1569:

At last, gentle people, here is the methodical disposition, so passionately wanted, so impatiently awaited, the hard-won redaction of the customs according to which our ancestors so happily administered public business. The customs here, of course, cost much time to lift from the dust; if so many thorns (that you know about) had not been met with, you would be right to be less pleased with your official, because, truth to tell, one is not at all indebted for what one has dragged out rather than received. But apart from the incredible work employed simply to set out various opinions so that they agree on the same matter, there was need of several Hercules to overcome the difficulties, common and frequent, as much in seeking out the

articles in each chapter, as in verifying them. This was not done by
giving way to the opinions of individuals, but by a precise and pain-
ful reading through of the judgments, memorials, and instructions
which mossy antiquity left in the strongboxes of the town. Despite
all this, the customs are dear to us for the utility the public will receive from them.

The Maître Echevin's words make clear both the great difficulty
of finding the customary law and the belief that it is embedded in
judicial decisions.

Brutails claimed, and he has recently been followed by Ourliac, that the idea of legality is very obscure in Andorran brains.[18]
Now if this means, as I think it does, that these scholars believe
that there is often great doubt in Andorra as to what legal rules
are appropriate to a given situation, and that ascertaining the
precise legal rule does not rank as a high priority in general
Andorran thinking, then their position should be generalized.
For obvious reasons, it is often the case in customary systems that
the legal rules are uncertain and that this is not treated as a matter
of great concern. Customary law most flourishes in small communities with a high degree of kinship, and the law is not an
academic learned law. Hence, to begin with, there will be a
relatively small number of disputes, and in a customary system,
disputes delimit the scope of legal rules. Again, in the necessary
absence of a strong academic tradition, there will be a reluctance
to generalize from the cases and extract principles which can be
used in other, rather different, situations. Moreover, what few
important decisions there are may not be adequately recorded or
be easily accessible. To give one example from a living customary
system: the first published Andorran decisions appeared in a
journal, *Revista jurídica de Cataluña*, only in 1963,[19] and there are
still only two collections in book form. That of Carles Obiols i
Taberner covers the years 1945 to 1966 and contains only
ninety-six appellate decisions.[20] That of Ourliac, already mentioned, also contains his commentary and covers decisions on
appeal to Perpignan for the years 1947 through 1970. Signifi-

cantly, both sets of reports occupy each only one fairly slim volume. Above all, there is relatively little demand for a precise knowledge of the legal rules in a customary system because so many disputes in the small community are among relatives, friends, or neighbors who have to live with one another afterwards and who therefore often have recourse to a less formal means of dispute-solving. Respected friends or relatives may be invited to adjudicate or there may arise in a village a recognized approach to adjudication. In any case, those appointed to judge will often decide by their opinion of what is fair and reasonable rather than search for a definite legal rule. Formal legal rules do not necessarily give the most acceptable solution. But if a problem situation occurs often enough, and if the same solution is usually reached (which need not be the case), a custom may emerge.

In the second place, often the customary law does not come from what the people do but is borrowed from elsewhere. The standard practice, particularly common in medieval France, of one jurisdiction accepting the law of another system as its residual custom is striking testimony to this, whether the outside system of the Coutume de Paris or of a neighboring custom, as in the *pays de droit coutumier* or of Roman law, as in the *pays de droit écrit*. This wholesale reception, though it is residual, is particularly revealing, both because it cuts down the discretionary choice in the individual situation and because the outside system may have originated for a very different society (in economic and political terms), such as ancient Rome, or for a much larger, more commercial, and more anonymous center, such as Paris. The same phenomenon occurs even when a local patriot prepares an unofficial collection of the customs. For instance, modern scholars agree that by far the greatest part of the *Conseil* of Pierre de Fontaines comes from Justinian's *Digest* and *Code*,[21] even though it was meant to be a practical work for training a friend's son in the local customs (*Conseil*, chap. 1, para. 2). The same can be said for the contemporary *Livre de Jostice et de Plet*, a product of the

Orleans area, where the Roman and canon law origins of the rules are hidden and ascribed falsely to French notables.[22] Of course, when these works were unofficial they would not themselves create the customary law, but they could be, and were, frequently treated by the courts as evidence of the custom. Here, too, court decisions have particular relevance: by adopting the rules in the books, whatever the origin of those rules, they declare the rules as custom. Again, in perplexing cases the courts themselves frequently based their decisions on customs from elsewhere. Thus, Philippe de Beaumanoir also wished to confirm part of his book "for doubtful cases in the said county, by judgments of neighboring lordships." Here not only was a "foreign" source of law borrowed, to be treated as the custom of the borrower,[23] but the borrowed foreign rule was actually that embedded in the foreign judgment. Again, the borrowed rule would have (at least in authority) the force of law only when it was incorporated in a judgment or judgments of the borrower.

Thus, it often happens that the acceptance of rules as local customary law comes from local judgments, and not from preceding local behavior.[24] When this happens, the basis of the law is treated as custom, not judicial precedent. What then is the role of judgments in creating customary law? The nature of the question becomes clear, and so perhaps does the answer, if we set out a series of propositions, beginning with those already established.

1. To be law custom needs more than behavior.
2. Opinio necessitatis fails to provide the extra factor.
3. Court decisions declare customary law even when (*a*) custom is uncertain (and there is no opinio necessitatis) and even when (*b*) there is no custom.
4. Proposition 3 is accurate even when (as in many systems) court decisions themselves do not make law; hence we cannot simply say the court decision is the basis of customary law.

5. Custom officially written down as law is law as statute, though that is not proof that the custom was not law before.

Propositions 1 to 4 have been established. Proposition 5 is self-evident. But we can now go on:

6. If court decisions are not law and therefore are not the basis of custom becoming law, but decisions declare custom as law even when there was no preceding practice (that is, taking propositions 3 and 4 together), then it is the official declaration of a rule as customary law that makes it law (whether the behavior was customary or not).

Therefore, it is official recognition that particular normative behavior is customary that makes it law. But official recognition also entails official acceptance. Hence, the validity of this custom as law depends on its official recognition and acceptance. The custom was not law before.

The objection may be made that though official recognition makes law as custom what was not the practice before, nonetheless habitual normative behavior may be law as custom even before official recognition, especially if the practice is universally regarded as the custom. The objection, though *prima facie* plausible, is ultimately untenable. Suppose a case involving the practice comes before the court and the court rejects the behavior as incorporating customary law; then one must hold that the custom cannot be law. Yet if the decision as decision does not create law, then it cannot be changing the law; hence the normative behavior was not customary law before the decision. It still remains that it is the official recognition of normative behavior as customary law that makes it law.

7. It follows that, in societies where customary behavior can be treated as law, there is an attribution to the people of

the power to make law by their tacit behavior, but this law is created only when it is officially recognized or accepted.

8. Just as the opinion of a sovereign is not law until it is institutionalized—as statute, for example—so behavior of the people is not law until it is institutionalized by being recognized and accepted by an official court decision.

"The will of the emperor has the force of statute" in Justinian's *Institutes* 1.2.6, means, as the text goes on to explain, that his will comes to have that effect when it is couched in the proper institutionalized form. "Deeply rooted custom is observed as a statute" (D.1.3.32.1) similarly means, as we have seen, that custom comes to have that effect when it is expressed in the proper institutionalized form, namely in judicial decision.

If the will of the emperor is mistakenly set out in the statute, it is the meaning that is accepted as being in the statute that prevails; likewise, if there was no custom, it is the meaning that is accepted as being in the judicial decision that prevails.

9. As a corollary, one might add that if custom has not been expressed in a judicial decision and hence is not law but is set out in an official redaction, it becomes law, but as statute, not custom.

On this understanding of the nature of customary law there is no difficulty either for its creation or alteration. Normative customary behavior becomes customary law when it is recognized by the courts as such. There is no need for a belief among the actors that they were already acting in accordance with an existing rule of law. So long as the courts treat the custom as law, it is the customary law, but should the courts hold that the custom has changed, then the new ruling becomes the customary law.

This leads on to the question—which, for our purposes, actually need not be asked—whether these findings might be used to support the theory of John Austin that law is the command of a sovereign which is backed by a sanction, when a sovereign is defined as someone whose commands are habitually obeyed and who is not in the habit of obedience to anyone else. At a first stage we should not be concerned with the validity of that theory as a whole, and we should for the sake of argument accept Austin's proposition that when judges make a legal rule, that rule is established by the sovereign legislature.[25] Our concern at this point is thus only with the question whether, if there can be no customary law without a court decision, that means that customary law is at least as much a command of the sovereign as binding precedent is.

Only three factual situations need be considered. First, it is argued by some writers, notably Vinnius,[26] that there can be no customary law under an emperor. Where there is an empire and this doctrine is accepted, there is no problem for Austin with regard to custom.[27] Second, where customary law is accepted and judicial precedent is binding, there is also no problem for Austin. One can say custom forms a rule of law because it is incorporated in a binding precedent. Third, where customary law is accepted and judicial precedent is not otherwise binding, the people as a whole is not the sovereign in Austin's sense. Their behavior makes law, but only at the moment when it is recognized and accepted by the court. That acceptance is necesary. Hence, insofar as Austin's argument is correct that court decisions accepted by the sovereign as creating law are commands of the sovereign, custom regarded as law when it is accepted as such by decision of the court is equally a command of the sovereign. The point is significant because, as we have seen, it is frequently urged that one of the major weaknesses in Austin's theory is precisely the difficulty of fitting customary law within it.[28]

But when one proceeds to a second stage, there remains a difficulty for accepting Austin's theory as a whole. Binding judicial precedent and customary law are on a level as forms of lawmaking in the sense that both require the consent, the acceptance, and the tolerance of the sovereign to be law. That consent, acceptance, and tolerance might be withheld. Nonetheless, it seems far-fetched to equate consent, acceptance, and tolerance with a command.

It seems to me that Austin is saying in effect that all law is legislation and that judges, insofar as they are lawmakers, are legislators. My position, I think, is different. I would accept that binding judicial precedent amounts to lawmaking in its own right—it is a source of law distinct from legislation—but it has the requirement that it be accepted by the sovereign as an appropriate method of creating law. Likewise, custom is a separate source of law distinct from both legislation and judicial precedent. But like judicial precedent, custom in order to make law has the requirement that it be accepted by the sovereign. As is the case both with legislation and with binding precedent, custom, to become law, has to be clothed with the requisite form (which marks its official acceptance by the sovereign). For custom this is indeed that it is incorporated in a judicial decision. But that custom as a means of making law is not simply subsumed into binding precedent is shown by the fact that a society might accept custom as law (when set out in a judicial decision) but deny lawmaking effect to precedent.

The conclusion—that to a great extent customary law does not derive from what the people of a locality habitually do and that official judicial decisions declare the law—may illumine other aspects of the issue.

To begin with, we can now understand the situation described by F. Pollok and F. W. Maitland (one which has long puzzled me), that in the Middle Ages, neighboring villages might be inhabited by persons of the same race, religion, and language, subject for centuries to the same economic conditions, yet have very different rules for the central institution of matrimonial property.[29] In fact, the villages may well have shared a number of ways of arranging family property holding, but in each village one way will have become fixed as law following upon judicial decisions. The final result in any one place will contain some element of the arbitrary.

Secondly, the common German medieval practice of one independent town which was governed by customary law selecting another as its "mother" town for settling disputed legal issues and submitting issues to the "mother"'s *Schöffen* (nonprofessional judge-jurists) takes on a different aspect.[30] However the question to the Schöffen might be framed, the "daughter" town was not really seeking to know its own customary practice. Rather, the daughter town had no custom or the custom was unsettled or unknown, yet the town because of this dispute wanted a ruling and preferred it to be given by the mother town, whether because the latter's Schöffen had high prestige or because the local Schöffen preferred to distance themselves from local disputes. The practice, in fact, is one particular example of the more general phenomenon that often there is a lack of interest in establishing the local custom. The frequency of borrowing another's custom (already adverted to) is itself an example of this lack of interest. The popularity of the *Sachsenspiegel* is a further illustration. This unofficial statement of practice in the bishoprics of Magdeburg and Halberstadt in the early thirteenth century was widely used in northern Germany, Poland, the Low Countries, and elsewhere. Of its two parts, one survives in over 200 manuscripts, the other in almost 150, and it was translated numerous times.[31]

Yet another example is the enormous length of time that occurred before French local customs were reduced to writing even after the royal command. The Ordinance of Montil-les-Tours of Charles VII of 1453 required the redaction of the customs in each district, but a century was required before most of the work was done.[32] The delay is to be explained not just by the magnitude and difficulty of the task, but by a frequent lack of interest in establishing the custom.

All this alerts us to a possible danger of interpretation. It is well-known that there are "families" of customary law. We should not therefore deduce that the members of one family group are closer in economic, social, and political structure to the other members than they are to members of other legal families. The legal family may result from the choice of legal approaches.

Finally, in this context, a further explanation is required for the fact that, in many territories in the Middle Ages, there was so little legislation on private law. The explanation so often given is that there were lacking great foci of centralized power and that kings and other magnates were weak.[33] For some places and times this may be a complete explanation, but often it clearly cannot be. To begin with, there are very many instances of magnates' granting charters to towns and of their issuing statutes on matters relating to public law. Clearly magnates often had the power to legislate. And we cannot say the magnates' power to legislate on private law was bitterly resented by the people, who were fiercely attached to their customs. As we have seen, frequently there was no great attachment to the customs.[34] The simplest explanation is that magnates were often not concerned to legislate private law for their subjects. Magnates frequently have more interesting, more exciting, and perhaps more important things to occupy their time.

Of course, to show that customary law often does not derive from preceding local behavior is not to claim that it never, or only infrequently, does. To a great extent, even if not to a commonly measurable extent, it must do so. But when we turn to the most notable attempts in the Middle Ages to treat customary attitudes as determining customary law, namely the *Weistümer* in Germany and the *enquête par tourbes* in France, we find striking confirmation of the main claims of this chapter.

A *Weistum* involved the fixing of the local law through persons sharing the same law, and this was performed by the posing of formal questions in the law and the giving of formal answers. Which persons were summoned varied from place to place. Often, some questions were left unanswered (some to be filled at a later date or by an *Oberhof*),[35] but the result was rather like a restatement or code. Weistümer collections are extant from the eleventh century. In the course of time the Weistümer had to be in writing, executed by a notary. Weistümer were prepared only at the smallest local level, that of the village.[36]

In medieval France, when a judge was unaware of an alleged custom, he had to inquire into its existence by an *enquête par tourbes*. This involved a number of persons of good repute—ten was established as the minimum within the ressort of the Parlement de Paris—who had the legal question put to them, deliberated, and then (as an ordinance of 1270 puts it) "they will say between whom they observed that custom, in what case, in what place, if there was a court decision and in what circumstances." Their reply, which was to be in writing and sealed, was given as one voice.[37]

The very attempt to try to find out by Weistümer or enquête par tourbes what the custom was, amply shows that particular behavior was not known to be law and accepted and practiced as law by the persons sharing the same law. Hence, here too we cannot regard opinio necessitatis as providing the factor needed to turn behavior into law. They both show that it was often difficult to know what the law was. As the Weistümer system indicates, in cases where answers were not given, there were gaps in the law even with regard to basic matters. The reduction of Weistümer to writing indicates an awareness that the law should be (at least relatively) fixed for the future, and is another indication of the awareness that knowledge of law could easily be lost. And, of course, under both systems, it would still be the case that if courts refused to recognize a custom as law and would not enforce it, then it would not be customary law.

The importance of courts in the development or recognition or statement of customary law ensures a significant role for the legal tradition, especially that of the judges, in shaping the law.

Customary Law Outside Europe

We have been looking only at European law, but I believe that at least the following propositions have general application.

1. The extent of a customary rule is frequently very unclear.
2. Cases often arise for which the preceding custom, or even whether there was a preceding custom, is quite uncertain, but judgments have to be given as if according to custom. In the absence of writing, customary rules have a relatively limited survival rate, since knowledge of them is uncertain.
3. The unofficial writing down of customary law will be treated as giving evidence—often of great weight—of the law.
4. Decisions of a tribunal, though not binding precedent, come to carry great weight as a statement of, or the best evidence for, a legal custom.
5. Customary behavior which will not be given support by a tribunal will not come to be accepted as having the normative status of customary law.
6. The combined effect of propositions 1 through 5 is that it is the official recognition of normative behavior as customary (whether it was or not) that makes it customary law. This is so even though official recognition of custom be not accepted in any jurisdiction as the basis of customary law's being law.
7. Borrowing from other legal systems is frequent.

Since I believe my view on the nature of customary law is largely original, I would not expect to find it set out thus in any treatise on, say, modern African customary law, or to appear to be acceptable to any author of a treatise. Yet much that is inherent in the principles does seem to be contained, implicitly perhaps, in statements about African law. I should like to quote from authorities whom I would not charge with agreeing with my principles. I will begin with J. F. Holleman, in his *Shona Customary Law:*

By far the greater part of the information so collected consisted of case material, the facts of which could be checked and cross-checked when necessary. The majority of these cases were supplied by alternating teams of carefully selected informants, practically all of them people who were taking an active part in the tribal administration of justice as assessors to a chief's or headman's court, and who could therefore quote from personal experience. A great number of cases I witnessed myself by regularly attending the sessions of the local tribal courts.

These actual cases formed a realistic basis for a discussion and analysis of the legal principles involved. As one case report led to another, and the pile of factual data grew, the various aspects of Shona law emerged, not as a clear pattern of strictly defined rules, but as a collection of broad concepts and guiding principles, the practical application of which varied with virtually every case in which they were reflected. Only in exceptional circumstances, when no actual cases could be supplied to illustrate certain points of law, were hypothetical cases submitted to different teams of informants in order to ascertain their views.

It thus became possible, on the basis of a vast stock of case material, not only to conceive and formulate the general principles of an indigenous system of law, but to reveal its great flexibility as one of its essential characteristics. This explains the collection of case reports included in this volume. They have been selected, not because they are always correct interpretations of Shona law (many of them are not), or because they carry the weighty authority of a legal precedent such as is found in our legal system (they are never, in fact, interpreted like that), but because they are illustrations of an indigenous administration of justice in which a satisfactory solution of the conflict between the parties often matters more than a correct interpretation of the legal principles involved.[38]

Next, from L. Shapera, *Handbook of Tswana Law and Custom:*

The Tswana themselves speak of their laws as having always existed,
from the time that man himself came into being;[39] or as having
been instituted by God *(Modimo)* or by the ancestor spirits *(badimo).*
This does not imply that no laws at all are held to have been made
by man. But it does serve to direct attention to one important fact:
the mechanism of the courts is used for the most part to enforce the
observance of usages which have already established themselves in
practice and become accepted through tradition. . . .

The existence of the courts has created another important source
of law, in the form of judicial decisions. The courts in the first place
must declare what the law is. A custom, until brought before them,
operates as part of the general system of behaviour incumbent upon
members of the tribe. If brought before the courts, and held to be
valid, it obtains recognition as good law, and henceforth is supported by the additional sanction of judicial enforcement. The courts
do not create the custom: they merely recognize, and by so doing
strengthen, the obligatory character of a rule already in existence.
Sometimes, however, the courts will hold that a custom, even if
generally observed, is incompatible with the existing conditions of
tribal life, and will refuse to regard it as legally binding. Here the
role of the courts in defining the law is even more apparent. Decisions of this nature have become fairly frequent as Western civi-
lization has penetrated more deeply into Tswana life.[40]

F. A. Ajayi writes of Nigeria:

In spite of both judicial and legislative attempts to ensure the development of customary law, there are still, as most people would
agree a number of *lacunae* in the whole system.[41]

Hans Cory declares in his *Sukuma Law and Custom:*

These variations [in law] had developed within the tribe primarily
because of its size. In times when communications between the pop-
ulated areas were poor, when permanent inter-tribal warfare existed, when wild animals endangered the life of the traveller, and
superstitious fear was dominant, exchanges of cultural achievements

were not common. Therefore, partly owing to the influence of neighbours in the boundary chiefdoms and partly through the action of autocratic rulers, laws underwent local changes. Many recent examples can be found where a chief has decided upon a beneficial change of anachronistic laws for his own area; such changes have seldom been accepted by others, even if their advantages were clear, because jealousy has been greater than insight.[42]

These quotations show that the authors are aware of one or more of the following: that there are important gaps in customary law; that customary legal rules are not clear or precise; that customary law is not easily known; that case law, though not binding as precedent, declares what the customary law is; that customary law can be affected by the influence of neighbors; that a powerful magnate can change or deliberately fail to change law; that courts may not accept customary behavior as law and it is then not law. That they do not seem to question that customary law exists even before it is declared by the courts is only to be expected given the traditional view of the nature of customary law.

Instances of the impact of Western law, even when it is not imposed, are too numerous and well-known to require exemplification.[43]

The very numerous restatements of tribal law, of which Cory's book is one,[44] have striking similarities to Weistümer: they betray the feeling that customary law requires to be (relatively) fixed for the future, and that it is easily lost. Restatements may be formed after inquiries similar to those used for Weistümer,[45] and then they bear similar implications.

III

The Cause of the Reception of Roman Law

From the eleventh century to the eighteenth and even beyond, the main feature of legal change in Western Continental Europe was the Reception of Roman law. At the beginning of that period law was above all custom, and throughout the period the main development in private law lay in the interaction between custom and Roman law. Certainly there were also statutes, but for private law they were relatively few, did not provide the main thrust of change, and were not at the center of legal interest. In their own spheres also, canon law and feudal law came to be supreme, but for convenience they may be left aside in this account, not least because to a considerable extent their history is also a parallel one of interactions with Roman law. The main question to be answered in Western legal history is an old one, one posed, for example, by Paul Vingradoff at the very beginning of his famous work, *Roman Law in Medieval Europe*.

Within the whole range of history there is no more momentous and puzzling problem than that connected with the fate of Roman Law after the downfall of the Roman State. How is it that a system shaped to meet certain historical conditions not only survived those conditions, but has retained its vitality even to the present day, when political and social surroundings are entirely altered? Why is it still deemed necessary for the beginner in jurisprudence to read manuals compiled for Roman students who lived more than 1500 years ago? How did it come about that the Germans, instead of working out their legal system in accordance with national precedents, and with the requirements of their own country, broke away from their historical jurisprudence to submit to the yoke of bygone doctrines of a foreign empire?[1]

The main thrust of this chapter is to explain the cause of this so-called "Reception" in the eleventh century. But some theorizing and earlier history are needed first. The theorizing now, to illuminate legal institutions as something different from, but related to, the corresponding social institutions; to illustrate the nature of legal ideas; and to account for legal borrowing from a society which has or had very different economic, social, religious, and political conditions and opinions. The earlier history, to show that the Reception was not a one-off thing, but corresponds to cultural rules of legal borrowing. The main issue, of course, is to explain how one system, Roman law, could have such an impact on so many others with such different contours. After all, the societies that gave rise to the law in the *Corpus Juris Civilis*, whether that of pagan Rome of the second century A.D. or that of Christian Constantinople of the sixth, were unlike the states of Western Europe in the eleventh and subsequent centuries; and they in turn could be very different from one another. And even earlier, the Germanic tribes which borrowed pre-Justinianic Roman law have always been considered to be very different from the Romans of their time in their mores, in their economic development, in their political structure, and in their religion.

Some Theory

Everyone would accept that, in the developed world, law is a separate entity in society, a distinct social institution. Yet somehow it is difficult to conceptualize legal ideas, in the way that one can conceptualize philosophical or religious ideas, as something different in kind from other ideas. The nature of the problem becomes apparent when we consider a legal institution, such as slavery for example. Slavery (when it exists) is a legal institution with a bundle of legal rules. Slavery is also a social/economic/political institution: for brevity I will use "societal" institution to express this notion. Whether a society accepts or rejects slavery will, of course, depend on societal circumstances. Slavery as a societal institution will not be brought into existence because a law of slavery exists or to complement a law of slavery. Rather, a law of slavery is wanted or needed because slavery is wanted or needed for societal reasons.[2] In other words, a legal institution is a social institution which has been given legal effectiveness and which is being regarded from the legal point of view. A legal institution, to be at all meaningful, depends on a societal institution.

But let us break down the legal institution of slavery. There are certain matters typically regulated by law, such as enslavement and manumission. Who is to become a slave—only persons of certain racial groups, only persons belonging to and captured from a foreign society which has no treaty of friendship, criminals convicted of particular offenses, children born to a slave mother—is an issue which will be resolved primarily by societal values. Likewise it is societal concerns which will determine whether any owner can free any slave, whether the owner or the slave has to be above a certain age for manumission, whether the consent of state authorities is required, whether an owner can free only *inter vivos* or by testament, whether there are restrictions on the number of slaves who can be freed, and the standing in the community of slaves who have been freed. At what level do legal ideas, if they are distinct from societal ideas, come in?

The problem may be approached by picturing a society that has as yet little in the way of law. Imagine that in the society the issue is raised for the first time whether an individual of a particular type is a slave. A decision will be reached on societal grounds (at least in the absence of a sophisticated legal analogy). Plus, perhaps, justice. But justice, too, is a societal notion, though it is or may be conceptually distinct from law. But if the issue is raised several times, or if in the first instance the ruling was treated as decisive for subsequent like cases, then there may in turn emerge, in a similarity of approach, a rule which can be termed a legal rule. What is a legal rule? At this level it is a crystallization of particular societal values organized so as to enable problems or disputes to be resolved with less trouble.

The means for resolving the disputes are also originally rooted in societal and not legal values. Judges will be those persons who are considered in societal terms to be fit to judge; what is regarded as probative will be determined by societal notions of proof. Likewise, legal rules will come into being in ways that have societal approval: if, for example, kings or councils have the requisite authority, they may make general declarations that will be regarded as creating legal rules.

Thus, legal institutions are societal institutions; the detailed rules derive from societal values; even the elements of the trial process and the ways of creating law will stem from societal facts.

Yet, even if we accept that the legal derives from the societal, it is prima facie obvious that law also exists as something distinct from other institutions in society. It is to some extent autonomous, and exists and operates within its own sphere. This we saw even in the first chapter. Law for our purposes may reasonably be regarded as the means adopted to institutionalize dispute situations and to validate decisions given in the process whose specific object is to inhibit further unregulated conflict.[3] The picture of law and society just given, if it is ever historically accurate, is so only at a very early stage. But when does law come to take on this life of its own, and cease to be simply a reflection of other aspects of society? First, it takes on this life of its own when factual situations come to be determined according to a standard, a standard which has emerged from the societal norm, but is treated as having its own existence. A standard implies some degree of uniformity, but what is involved is rather more. Uniformity, for instance, in deciding similar cases in the same way may result from a consideration of the societal factors. But there is determination according to a standard when judges wish to give the same results in suits which have similar facts *primarily because* of the other rulings and when a ruler announces that whenever and as often as a named factual situation arises, he will do or cause to have done some particular thing. That is to say that determination according to a standard involves a kind of shorthand. A solution to a problem is to be arrived at by the application of the shorthand: the individual societal factors which previously would have been taken into account are not resorted to; the standard, which is in effect a legal rule, has usurped the role of the societal factors. The main reasons for this occurring are plain. To begin with, it makes the decision-making much simpler: the obvious efficiency is enhanced when one takes into account that the standard can be regarded as the crystallization of the societal factors. Again, the existence of a standard gives greater certainty for regulating the future. Thirdly, the application of a standard does, as it is meant to, lead to some equivalence of treatment which gives at least the appearance of one kind of justice. Fourthly, the party against whom the judgment is given will accept it more readily, feel less aggrieved, if he thinks a standard is being applied and the judge is not arbitrary.

But whenever and wherever this happens there ceases to be a necessary, entire congruence between the standard and society. With regard to decision-making, the standard—that is, the legal rule—now stands in the stead of all the societal factors once thought relevant. Societal factors may change without a corresponding change in the standard. Or the standard may have been imposed because of a very temporary situation which may have concerned the whole society or only a segment. Or the standard may have been formulated inexactly or in a primitive way for the societal conditions of the time. In any event, the very erection of a standard amounts to proof that societal values may not prevail in a particular case. Judging is to be in accordance with the standard. It is precisely the standard that is to prevail.

A standard according to which determination should be made is not to be equated with what happens in practice in court. In practice a great deal may happen in court that has nothing to do with the standard and is even extralegal: for instance, bribery of a witness or of the judge. Or again the standard may exist prior to any court deliberation: for instance, a statute may set out rules which will be obeyed, which will have an impact, before there is any question of a process. Further, to give a concrete example, the Roman jurists created the standards by their writings and discussions, but they seem to have been quite indifferent to what happened in court.

Further (and it is almost simply the other side of the coin), law takes on a life of its own whenever and wherever the decision is regarded as authoritative, not because it is thought necessarily to encapsulate societal values but because the judge is treated as the right person to give the decison—in other words, when the authority of the decison derives from the way the judge is appointed and from the fact that he has followed the procedures of judging rather than from the intrinsic quality of the decision. The judgment can be appealed only to a higher judge, and the authority of his decision rests on his senior status, not on his necessarily being better acquainted with societal values.[4]

On the model so far proposed, legal rules and deliberations are purely the result of societal ideas even though the stage may be reached that the legal rules do not by any means exactly fit the dominant societal ideology. The reason is apparent: law is not an end in itself but is always a means to other ends.

But the model so far proposed is obviously oversimple in another way. The ends may be societal ends, but the means to the ends require human ingenuity, and they inevitably involve standards having a distinct status. In addition, in the Western tradition at least, law becomes the province of specialized groups who may loosely be termed lawyers.[5] Lawyers themselves may be divided into groups, and in every society there will be one or more elite legal groups who to a very great extent control lawmaking or law-finding. Legal ideas and legal tradition result from the amalgam of law as (*a*) involving standards having a distinct status, (*b*) human ingenuity, and (*c*) an elite making or finding the standards, all dependent on societal ends which may to some extent be not expressed, or be forgotten or ignored.

The elite of lawmakers or law-finders must be emphasized. They become so involved with law as law that they often talk of it as if it existed for its own sake, and they cease to regard it—or at least to treat it—as existing for specific societal purposes. Thus, the Roman jurist Julian, of the second century A.D., claims (and he is talking about law): "The reason cannot be given for all matters established by our ancestors"; and this text is followed in Justinian's *Digest* by one of Neratius, who is slightly earlier: "And therefore it is not proper to seek the reasons of those matters that are established, for otherwise many of those things that are certain are overturned" (D.1.3.20, 21). In the eighteenth century, in his *Institutions du droit belgique* (1736), George de Ghewiet, who refers with approval to those Roman jurists, also says: "On this principle one must stop at the provisions of the homologated customs without worrying about the *why*. It is enough that they are as we find them" (1.1.5.2). In the twentieth century it is still the typical practice for the authors of English legal textbooks not to give the reason for the rules that they set out.

The notion that the law and the legal tradition powerfully affect the way the law develops is one that I have argued for on several occasions elsewhere,[6] and it appears prominently in Chapter 1. Here the reminder of one example from that chapter may suffice. Barter as a societal institution will exist in many societies, but not all such societies will recognize a contract of barter. Thus the city of Rome was traditionally founded in 753 B.C. (and may be older), and a contract, the stipulatio, was well-established by 451 B.C., the date of the codification known as the Twelve Tables. Coined money was introduced in the third century B.C., and the consensual contract of sale, *emptio venditio*, followed hard upon. Yet, as we saw barter, *permutatio*, as a legal institution is centuries later, and it was never fully accepted into the Roman system of contracts. As a contract it was very unsatisfactory; the Sabinians tried to include it within the satisfactory contract of sale but were blocked by the successful counterarguments of the Proculians. Neither side used societal arguments. Law was being treated as if it were an end in itself. In these circumstances only the most blinkered modern ideologue would deny that just as mercantile needs to some extent shape legal development so the existing law to some extent shapes mercantile practices. It would be a grave mistake to suppose that because the mercantile elite can take more advantage than others of the law that the law is necessarily shaped to their advantage.

Legal rules and the legal tradition are therefore separated from society though connected with it. The legal tradition as something distinct is most obvious in two spheres: first, in societal institutions which appear to require support as legal institutions but do not receive it; second, in categorization, in the drawing of boundary lines, whether in the boundaries between two clearly defined, separate legal institutions such as barter and sale, or in determining whether one or more legal institutions is to provide for what may be regarded as more than one societal or legal institution, as in the hire of a thing, hire of labor, hire of work to be done.

This separation of law from, but partial dependence on, societal institutions must be stressed. The law created by a society for its use is often by no means a perfect fit. And the historical reasons for the precise contours of the legal institution may well be forgotten. Yet people for the most part accept the law they have. They do not demand perfection. All this is a necessary precondition for one of the strangest of legal phenomena: the prodigious extent of legal borrowing. We need not concern ourselves here with the other prerequisites for successful legal transplants. It is enough to know that transplants occur in great number, that the recipient society may have very different values from the donor, and that the reasons justifying the acceptance of the foreign law may be different from those that created it in the first place. A general example for the above propositions is provided by the influence of the French *Code Civil* throughout the world;[7] a particular example, by the enshrinement of the Visigothic law of matrimonial property in the constitution of California,[8] and its acceptance in several German states (before unification) and Latin American countries. Societies with systems of customary law also frequently resort to extensive borrowing. To prove this it is enough to point to the enormous popularity of the *Sachsenspiegel*, an early-thirteenth-century account of the law of a part of East Saxony which was used throughout northern Germany and far beyond; to the adoption by medieval German towns of another as their "mother" town on points of law (Magdeburg is the supreme example, but others, too, had many "daughters"; thus, Lübeck had about 100 and Soest, 65); and to the frequent acceptance in medieval French jurisdictions of the law of another, frequently Paris, as subsidiary law whenever the local custom failed to provide an answer.[9]

If it is the case that legal ideas evolve from societal ideas, yet come to have a (semi-) independent but subordinate existence; if, moreover, societal ideas and practices can exist without corresponding law; if the corresponding law may be inadequate; if one societal institution may be divided arbitrarily between more than one legal institution, each with its own imperfections; if several societal institutions may be brought within the same legal institution because of the legal tradition; but if, still, the subordination of law continues; and if, further, one can accept that with law in general, and also with customary law, borrowing is at least one of the most fruitful sources of legal development— then even on a priori grounds one can set out some general propositions about the grafting of Roman law onto customary systems.

To start with the extreme position. It would seem at first glance that there can be no transplanting of the legal institution where the possible donor's societal institution is the reverse of the recipient's societal institution. For example, a society having a system of bride price but not of dowry will not (or is not very likely to) borrow the corresponding law from a society having a system of dowry but not of bride price. But this immediately invites and even demands serious qualification. If the societal institution of dowry is not adopted, then the central core of the law of dowry also will not be borrowed; but surrounding rules may be, and then be attached to bride price: rules such as those determining the amount to be paid, the times for payment, and the rights of retention if the marriage fails. But this borrowing of these surrounding rules implies some degree of precision and clarity in the donor system and a felt need, which may be real or imaginary, in the recipient system. Hence, in general this type of borrowing implies greater precision and clarity in the donor. Borrowing of this type, of surrounding rules but not of the central core of the legal institution because the societal institutions are very different, will generally be from the more advanced by the less advanced. But the recipient need take only what it requires at any one time. Hence the reception can take a very long time.

If the outline just given is accurate, then we have the beginnings of an explanation of some phenomena of the Reception of Roman law into customary systems. First, many different systems can all be borrowers from the same source: each takes, or need take, only what it wants, irrespective of the borrowings of others. Secondly, the pace of the Reception varies from place to place: each system takes only when it needs or wants. Thirdly, systems of customary law are peculiarly susceptible to this type of borrowing from elsewhere precisely because they are notoriously lacking in precision and clarity: when a need for a rule arises it may not be found or easily found in what the people do.

Fourthly, a sophisticated system of Roman law may exist and be studied extensively in a society whose main law is customary. The main advantage of this for the society at large, as distinct from the professors of Roman law, is precisely that Roman law may be called upon to fill gaps in the customary system. Of course, where the societal institution in the two societies is very similar, the borrowing even of the central core of the legal institution from the more advanced legal system is easier, especially if the borrower's legal institution has not developed at all or only very partially.

In fact, the tenor of the foregoing paragraph is almost entirely encapsulated by a seventeenth-century judge and jurist, Lord Stair, in his *Institutions of the Law of Scotland*, 1.1.15 (1st ed., 1681):

> *Our Customes*, as they have arisen mainly from Equity, so they are also from the Civil Canon and Feudal Laws,[10] from which the Terms, Tenors and Forms of them are much borrowed; and therefore these especially (the Civil Law) have great weight, namely in cases where a custome is not yet formed; but none of these have with us the Authority of Law.

Here we have the frank declaration that in Scotland customary law is often borrowed—especially when a Scottish custom is not yet formed—from a more developed system that is also accessible in writing; that even where there is a local custom, it will come to be expressed in the terminology of the donor system and given its form and also its content; and that the borrowing is optional, though some outside systems will be particularly persuasive. If one can extrapolate from Scotland, as I think one properly can, then other countries differing in their societal structure would likewise borrow what they needed. The borrowing could be little by little, when an individual problem arose. To illustrate the process, an example from another Scottish attorney's speech to the court is quoted and discussed in Chapter 4.

Some History

I propose now to look at two extensive instances of legal borrowing before the Reception of Roman law which began in the
eleventh century. The first is the influence of pre-Justinianic
Roman law on Germanic customs that becomes very apparent
from the fifth century. The second is the spread of Visigothic law
throughout Spain under and after Moorish domination. I am not
outlining this history for its own sake but to show that the more
famous Reception corresponds to the same cultural rules of legal
borrowing, and hence that the explanation of its occurrence
presents no special problems. The argument here rests on an
acceptance of the principle known as "Ockham's Razor," whether
that principle be expressed as "Plurality is not to be assumed
without necessity" or "What can be done with fewer is done in
vain with more." Thus, if the borrowing of pre-Justinianic law
by the Germanic tribes, the acceptance of Visigothic law by the
Christian communities in Spain, and the Reception of Roman
law are similar in their essentials, then a satisfactory general
causative explanation of one ought to be a satisfactory general
causative explanation of the others. There will, of course, also be
individual causes of borrowing in each instance.

For the influence of Roman law on Germanic customs I should
like to start with the *Edictum Theoderici*,[11] treating it as the oldest
surviving example and as the work of the Visigothic king Theoderic II (453–66). There are various reasons for this course of
action. First, though there is no agreement as to the author,
Theoderic II (or Magnus of Narbo, the *praefectus praetorio Galliarum* of his time)[12] seems to be the current favorite. Secondly, I
believe he is the most likely candidate. Thirdly, the course of
influence of Roman law is most simply explained if we begin
with him. Fourthly, this starting point, as we shall see, is the least
helpful for my general thesis.

The other main contender for the authorship of the edict has
always been Theoderic the Great, king of the Ostrogoths

(493–526), who was supported by the first editor, Pierre Pithou in 1579, who had at his disposal two manuscripts that have now disappeared. Against this identification is the fact that though his reign is well-documented, he is never cited by contemporaries as responsible for a legal compilation—not by Cassiodorus, Jordanes, Epiphanius, Ennodius, Procopius, or others. Moreover the Imperial constitutions are cited in the *Edictum* for no date later than 458. For Theoderic II of the Visigoths, on the other hand, speaks this dating of the constitutions in the *Edictum* and the fact that Sidonius Apollinaris says that Seronatus—usually thought to be *praefectus praetorio Galliarum* or governor of Aquitanica Prima around 469 or holder of some other office, it does not matter which—tramples on the laws of Theodosius and issues laws of Theoderic.[13] One might also want to give some weight to Sidonius's claim (*Car.* 7.495f.) that, thanks to Avitus, the laws of Rome had long appealed to Theoderic II; and perhaps even some to the obvious fact that of all the Germanic peoples, the Visigoths showed most interest in law and also borrowed most from Roman law.[14] For our present purposes it would not matter whether one said that Theoderic II issued the *Edictum* or Magnus of Narbo as the Roman magistrate or, as Vismara hypothesizes, that Magnus was the jurist entrusted by Theoderic to draft the *Edictum*.[15] It should be noted, though, that the text of Sidonius treated as indicating Magnus's authorship (*Car.* 5.561f.) seems to be misunderstood and must actually refer to Theoderic. Sidonius's poem is a panegyric on Majorian, and in stressing the good qualities of the emperor's assistants, he has just referred to the prefect: "qui dictat modo iura Getis, sub iudice vestro pellitus ravum praeconem suspicit hostis" ("The enemy dressed in skins, who now gives law to the Goths, under your judgeship, admires the hoarse auctioneer"). But he who now gives law to the Goths (*qui dictat modo iura Getis*) must grammatically and logically be the enemy dressed in skins (*pellitus hostis*), who cannot be Magnus and must be the king of the Visigoths.

The *Edictum* consists of 154 provisions plus a prologue and epilogue. The immediate purpose—irrespective of any wider political motive—was to set out, as the prologue and epilogue expressly state, the legal rules that were to apply both to Romans and Goths.[16] Thus not all of the law was covered. But what is remarkable is that with this purpose the provisions all seem to have a Roman origin, whether in juristic writing or in imperial rescripts.[17] Many of the provisions relate to criminal law and punishment, others to such diverse topics as testation, gifts, transfer of property, slavery, and marriage.

This purpose and the scope of the rules give a straight, conclusive answer to at least one possible puzzle: why the earliest collection of legal rules applying to a Germanic tribe were written in Latin, thus setting a trend that was to continue. This approach renders unnecessary a further explanation[18] which may nonetheless have some validity: that the Germanic languages did not have the vocabulary needed to cope with law. If we give some credence to this idea, it further entails holding that the *Edictum* is giving a precision to the Germanic customs that was previously lacking. In any event, the use of Roman vocabulary means that, in Stair's words, "the terms, tenors, and forms of them [i.e. Roman legal institutions] are much borrowed."[19] Although we have no real evidence for the previous state of the Visigothic law, it would be a remarkable coincidence if so much Roman law was also common to the Visigoths. We have here, in all probability, a massive transplant.

On the view here proposed, the term *Edictum* would be used either technically or at least figuratively. Roman public officials did not have the power to legislate, but they could declare by *edicta* how they would carry out their duties. Above all, the Republican praetors, the officials in charge of the most important courts of private law, issued annual *Edicta* setting out the circumstances in which they would grant an action.[20] Thus the *Edictum Theoderici* is not *lex*, statute law. Only the emperor could issue statutes for Roman citizens. The term *Edictum* is very appropriate for legal rules that apply to Romans as well as Goths, set forth by someone other than the emperor, though we do not know that Theoderic had any legal right to issue an edict in the technical sense. If the lines from Sidonius about Theoderic that have just been quoted do refer to the *Edictum Theoderici*, we have the beginning of an understanding of the obscure phrase *sub iudice vestro*. Theoderic is giving law—*iura* not *leges*—to the Goths with the emperor as his judge, or with the emperor's judicial representative in charge of court procedure. Whatever translation is appropriate the implication is the same: the law of Theoderic is subject to the emperor.

Whatever the nature of the *Edictum Theoderici* and its origins, the Visigoths soon had another code of laws. This is the *Codex Euricianus*, which has reached us only in part and is the work of Euric (466–84), successor to Theoderic II as king of the Visigoths. According to Isidorus of Seville (*Hist. Goth.* 35, written in 624), the Goths first obtained written laws under Euric and previously lived according to their customs. It is usually thought, however, that at least individual laws were promulgated under Theoderic I and Theoderic II. The *Codex* is dated to 475 or 476, immediately after the fall of the Roman Empire in the West.[21]

Insofar as the *Codex Euricianus* survived, it has been in the *Antiqua* (the "old texts" in the later *Visigothic Code*) and in a fragmentary palimpsest containing chapters 276–336.[22] The work is in Latin, and it has long been recognized that the law has been heavily Romanized. This is also the conclusion of Alvaro d'Ors, the most recent editor, who has also produced a palingenesia, though he does find details and traces of Germanic law.[23] Thus, the oldest surviving corpus of law produced for Germans was very much the result of massive borrowing. In its turn, it was to be very influential, and even serve as model for other Germanic codes (even apart from those of the Visigoths). Clear traces of it are found in law for the Franks in the *Lex Salica* of Chlodwig (486–511); for the Burgundians in the *Lex Gundobada*, which seems to be not before 483; for the Lombards in the *Edictum Rothari* of 643; and above all, for the Swabians in the *Lex Baiuwariorum* of the eighth century.[24]

In 506, another Visigothic king, Alaric II, produced a very different legal work, the *Breviarium Alaricianum* or *Lex Romana Visigothorum*. This work, which has survived, does not contain the laws of Visigothic kings, but Roman imperial constitutions and writings from Roman jurists. It is usually thought to have been issued with a political motivation: to try to retain the loyalty of Alaric's Gallo-Roman subjects who were Catholics—the Visigoths were Arians—and inclined to join with the Franks. The *Breviarium* was to provide some materials for the *Visigothic Code*. But more significantly, it served as a vehicle for the dissemination of law, and hence of Roman law, for many centuries in France. Its influence can be shown in the style of documents, in the redaction of formularies, and in conciliar canons from the sixth to the ninth centuries. In the eighth century especially there were numerous epitomes, and from the sixth to the tenth centuries legal science in France was largely restricted to using extracts from these epitomes and the Theodosian Code.[25]

The traditional view long held was that the Visigoths operated a system of personal, not territorial, law and hence that the *Codex Euricianus* was meant only for the Visigoths, the *Breviarium Alaricianum* only for the Romans living under Visigothic control. This view was challenged in 1941 by Alfonso García Gallo, who maintained that the Visigoths operated a system of territorial law and thus both the *Codex Euricianus* and the *Breviarium Alaricianum* (and other legislation) applied to Visigoths and Gallo- or Hispano-Romans alike: hence the *Codex Euricianus* was abrogated by the *Breviarium*.[26] A lively debate has followed,[27] no consensus has been reached, but there is now considerable agreement that the *Codex Euricianus* was territorial, as, according to common belief, was probably the *Breviarium*, though more doubt is expressed on this second point.[28]

The arguments thought persuasive for the territoriality of the *Codex Euricianus* are its profound Romanization and its edictal character.[29] Evidence of the edictal character of the work seems to me to be lacking, since we do not have the formulas of its promulgation, and other explanations of the Romanization can be provided. The general correctness of the traditional view I would maintain for the following reasons.[30] First, it is no real explanation of the profound Romanization that the code was meant to apply to Romans as well as to Visigoths and thus is a hybrid. The latter had just achieved political domination over the Romans. Why should they, to keep the Romans content, adopt for themselves as well a system based on Roman law? The Visigoths' adoption of Romanized law can only have occurred because the Visigoths themselves (or their leaders) wanted it as law: hence, an explanation extending its operation to Romans is unnecessary. Secondly, the *Breviarium* contains only Roman law texts and no laws of Visigothic kings. It is inconceivable that with this scope it was intended as law for the Visigoths as well, replacing the *Codex Euricianus*, especially in view of known Visigothic legislation. That the Visigoths had their own legal tradition is evidenced both by the prior *Codex Euricianus* and the subsequent *Visigothic Code*.

An alternative approach is to claim that the *Breviarium* did not derogate from the *Codex Euricianus* but was a work complementary to the *Codex*, "a subsidiary source principally destined for the Roman population."[31] The first part of that claim is easily admitted. Alaric begins the *Commonitorium* to Thimotheus: "Utilitates populi nostri propitia divinitate tractantes hoc quoque, quod in legibus videbatur iniquum meliore deliberatione corrigimus, ut omnis legum Romanarum et antiqui iuris obscuritas adhibitis sacerdotibus ac nobilibus viris in lucem intelligentiae melioris deducta resplandeat ac nihil habeatur ambiguum unde se diuturna aut diversa iurgantium impugnet obiectio ("We, in this also considering the advantage of our people with the help of God, correct after better deliberation what seemed unjust in statute law, so that all the obscurity of Roman statutes and of the ancient law, brought forth with the help of priests and honorable men into the light of better understanding, shines forth and contains nothing ambiguous, and hence the continuous and opposing squabbles of those who quarrel reduce themselves to naught"). Thus, any derogation is expressly from the preceding Roman *leges* and *ius*. But this is precisely what one would expect if the *Breviarium* was intended solely for the Roman population to whom the *Codex Euricianus* did not apply. The game is up for the claim of territoriality as soon as it has to be suggested that the *Breviarium Alaricianum* was destined principally for the Roman populace. How could it be, if one law applied to all? And if it were complementary to the *Codex*, which applied to both people, but the *Breviarium* was mainly for the Romans, why was the Visigoths' own law not given equal supplementation? If the ground of the argument were to be changed to the proposition that the *Codex Euricianus* and the *Breviarium* were territorial and that the latter was complementary for Romans and Visigoths alike, then we would be faced with an acute form of the converse of the issue which led to the notion of territoriality of Visigothic law: the Romanization. If the serious Romanization of the *Codex Euricianus* leads to the belief that it must have been intended for Roman and Visigoth alike, can the total Romanization of the *Breviarum* lead to the belief that it also must have been intended for Roman and Visigoth alike? And how can one then explain the subsequent serious Visigothization of the *Visigothic Code*?

Thirdly, if at this time Visigothic law was personal and the *Codex Euricianus* was promulgated for the Visigoths, the *Breviarium* for the Romans, then we would have almost an exact parallel from another Gothic people, the Burgundians. As we shall see, Gundobad, king of the Burgundians from 474 to 516, was responsible for the *Lex Burgundionum* (or *Lex Gundobada*) for his Burgundian subjects (and for conflict cases between Burgundian and Gallo-Roman) and the *Lex Romana Burgundionum* for his Gallo-Roman subjects.

Other Visigothic legislation followed. Teudis, king from 531 to 548, promulgated in 546 a law on procedural costs and ordered that it be included in the corresponding part of the *Breviarium*. Thus, the law was territorial, but the order to include it in the *Breviarium* would seem to indicate both that laws were not automatically for both peoples, and also that the *Breviarium* was not.

Leovigild (568–86) revised the *Codex Euricianus*, adding, cutting out, and modifying laws. This work has not survived in its own right. Subsequent kings, especially Chindasvind (642–53) and his son Recesvind (653–72), also legislated. But the most important work of Visigothic law was Recesvind's compilation of laws which had been promulgated until 654, the *Liber iudiciorum* or *Liber iudicum* or *Visigothic Code*. This massive compilation in twelve books, like Justinian's *Code* (though it is not certain that the compilers used that work),[32] replaced earlier law and was intended for all the people in the territory subjected to Visigothic domination. Roman law is the predominant element. Subsequent kings continued to legislate. Ervigius (680–87) revised the *Liber iudiciorum*, introducing many statutes of his own and of Wamba, correcting and interpolating earlier laws. Egica (687–702) intended a new revision: we do not know if this was carried out, but statutes of his were included. In addition to the official versions, anonymous jurists produced private, vulgarized versions with a new preliminary title. The result was the version known as the *vulgata*, which was the most widespread in the High Middle Ages. This legislative activity of the Visigoths came to an end in 711 with the conquest by the Moors.

Savigny places the texts of the *Liber iudiciorum* that reproduce Roman law in three categories.[33] First, there are those that reproduce Roman sources textually—for instance, on degrees of relationship, legitimate defense, and interest.[34] Secondly, very many texts reproduce Roman principles that have been adopted, imagined, modified, or completely changed. Savigny gives examples from the law of persons and related rules in succession.

The *Visigothic Code* 3.12 permits, with the authorization of the count, marriage between Goth and Roman. The prohibition is in *Codex Theodosianus* 3.14.1. A law that nuptial gifts by the husband may be equalled by the amount of the dowry is said to be that permitted by Roman law (*L. Visigoth* 3.1.6). Another law forbids remarriage during the year of mourning (3.2.1), a rule that is found in more than one of the Roman sources. A widow becomes tutor of her children.[35] Minority ends at the age of twenty-five (*L. Visigoth* 4.3.1), capacity to make a will begins at fourteen (2.5.10), and spouses inherit from one another in the absence of relatives (4.2.11). Manumission of slaves may take place in church.[36] Thirdly, some rules seem to be borrowed indirectly from Roman law by means of the *Lex Baiuwariorum*.

During the period covered by the foregoing summary the Visigoths were on the move. In 412, under Athaulf, they left Italy, which they had exhausted, and settled in Gaul. After many quarrels they entered Roman service and fought and defeated the Siling Vandals and the Alans in Spain. From there they were withdrawn to settle as federates in Aquitania in 418. In 435 a peasant revolt in Gaul gave the Visigoths (and the Burgundians) the opportunity to expand. From time to time the Visigoths intervened south of the Pyrenees, and apparently in 457, a relatively large number of Visigothic peasant families settled in the Tierra de Campos. Euric himself seems to have wanted to extend Visigothic rule over the whole of Gaul and Spain. He extended the Visigothic kingdom in Gaul so that it was bounded by the Loire, the Rhine, and the Pyrenees. Southern Provence also came under his control. Within the Visigothic and Burgundian kingdoms the confiscation of land was more drastic than in other territory controlled by other barbarians; in the *Codex Euricianus* the Visigoths took two-thirds, the Roman owner retaining only one-third. This rule was retained in subsequent legislation. In time the Visigoths had to face war with the Franks, and Alaric II was defeated and killed at the battle of Vouillé (near

Poitiers). Then followed a massive immigration of the Visigoths into Spain, always suffering further displacement to the south until Leovigild (568–86) situated his capital in Toledo.

Before we look at other Germanic codifications we should perhaps pause to consider some of the implications of the Visigothic experience. Visigothic law was the best developed of all Germanic laws, but what is most striking is the massive Romanization at an early stage, as early indeed as the *Codex Euricianus*, and so massive that modern legal historians are unwilling to believe that it was intended by the Visigothic king for the Visigoths alone. For the sake of the argument let us assume that it was also intended to apply to the Gallo- or Hispano-Romans under Visigothic rule. This would in no way diminish the impact of Roman law on the Visigoths, an impact they accepted freely, at their king's free choice. And the Romanization continued to increase even until the *Liber iudiciorum* itself. We began by accepting that the starting point for the codification was in the *Edictum Theoderici*, which we treated as representing an edict of a Roman magistrate setting out the law that applied to Romans and Visigoths alike. This made it easier to understand why Latin was the language—which could be thought to set the tradition—and why the law was Roman. But a beginning of this type does not explain why then or subsequently the Visigoths borrowed so much law from Rome. The borrowing continued over a long period of time. And it should again be stressed that Visigothic social mores, political structure, economic conditions, and religion were, and have always been accepted as being, vastly different from the Roman society for which Roman law was created.

But just as other societal conditions were very different among the Romans and the Visigoths, so were the systems of law at the beginning of this reception: not just in substance but in structure—custom as distinct from written law—and in the amount of detail and sophistication. Writing of the Germanic tribes in general at the time of the codification of their laws (and not excluding the Visigoths), the famous French legal historian A. Esmein follows the opinion of Sir Henry Maine: "Germanic law, at the period of the *Leges barbarorum*, was less advanced in its development than Roman law at the time of the Twelve Tables,"[37] that is, in the mid-fifth century B.C. Yet borrowing was not only possible but also massive.

The Burgundians were a second Gothic group prominent in code-making. The *Lex Burgundionum*—also called, for instance, the *Lex Gundobada*—an official collection of royal Burgundian laws, is mainly the work of King Gundobad, who ruled from 474 to 516. There are thirteen surviving manuscripts, none earlier than the ninth century; and of these, five have a text of 105 titles, the others having only 88 or a number of appendices. The work, in fact, is a composite, of which the first 88 titles comprise an earlier stage. Two manuscripts contain a short preface in which Gundobad claims to have given great thought to the laws of himself and his predecessors. Then follows in all manuscripts a heading to the effect that King Sigismond issued a new edition of the code in 517, the second year of his reign.[38] Of the first 88 titles, 2–41 stand together as the work, though revised, of Gundobad; 42–88 are rather different and stem from Sigismond. Title 1 has certainly been revised. Whether there are laws older than the time of Gundobad in the code is not certain.[39]

The date of the *Lex Burgundionum* is not known. It was intended to apply to the Burgundians, and in lawsuits between Burgundians and Romans. The Roman subjects of King Gundobad were to continue to be ruled by Roman law, and the preface expressly states that the Romans should know they will receive their own law book so that ignorance will excuse no one.[40]

The *Lex Burgundionum* contains many rules of Roman law, whether drawn directly or indirectly from Roman sources. Thus, a woman married for a second time retains only a usufruct of the gift given in contemplation of the first marriage, and ownership of it goes to the children (*L. Burg.* 24.1; *C. Th.* 3.8.2). The title on divorce is contradictory, but the provisions of 34.3, 4 permit a husband to divorce his wife if she is guilty of adultery, witchcraft, or violation of a tomb; if he leaves her otherwise, his property is forfeit to his wife and children. This is ultimately derived from the *Codex Theodosianus* 3.16.1, but the provisions there referred to divorce by a wife. Gifts and wills become valid provided five or seven witnesses append their marks or signatures (*L. Burg.* 43.1), a formality established by *Codex Theodosianus* 4.4.1 for the validity of wills and codicils. The requirement of an *inscriptio* in criminal charges also comes from Roman law.[41] The title on prescription, number 79, seems much influenced by Roman law; the legal treatment of documents comes from Roman vulgar law, and two texts show the use of the Roman vulgar law *Interpretationes*.[42] For Otto Stobbe this influence is explained by the fact that the *Lex Burgundionum* was intended to apply to Romans as well as to Burgundians (of course, only where there was a process between a Burgundian and a Roman).[43] But this explanation will not serve. There are two Burgundian codes, one for Burgundians, one for Romans. Each should contain what is appropriate for each people. There will be cases of conflict of law. If one set of rules is chosen to settle such issues we could reasonably expect it to be the Burgundian, since the Romans were the subject people. Roman rules in the Burgundian code which would also apply in cases where all interested parties were Burgundians cannot be explained on this basis. The reason for their presence simply must be that they are wanted by the Burgundians themselves. It seems as if legal historians like Stobbe are unwilling to believe the ease with which Roman legal rules could be accepted by the Germanic tribes.

But just as interesting, and possibly even more significant, are the numerous borrowings in the *Lex Burgundionum* from Visigothic law, and in fact from the *Codex Euricianus*. The borrowings are shown from the parallelisms or similarities in the *Antiqua* texts in the *Liber iudiciorum*, or in the *Lex Baiuwariorum*, which itself borrowed from the *Codex Euricianus*, or in the *Lex Salica* or the Lombard *Edictum Rothari*, which also were influenced by Visigothic law.[44]

The *Lex Burgundionum* remained in force after Burgundy became part of the empire of the Franks, and it is mentioned as personal law in documents of the tenth and eleventh centuries.

Gundobad's *Lex Romana Burgundionum* for his Roman subjects contains no new law but only that from Roman *ius* and *leges* and from the *Lex Gundobada*. It was not a complete account of Roman law, so that the Roman subjects also had to make use of the collections of imperial rescripts and juristic writings. Hence it lost most of its significance when the *Breviarium Alaricianum*, which was intended to be complete, became known in Burgundy. It has often been rightly stressed that to a great extent the Roman law that was the source of borrowing was not the pure, classical Roman law but the simplified law for the conditions of the time, known as Roman vulgar law.[45] It is easily conceivable that borrowing would become difficult if the cultural level of the source system was so high above that of the possible borrower that its law was virtually incomprehensible. But what matters to us here is simply that Roman vulgar law was in fact much more sophisticated and developed than Germanic customs, and still could be borrowed.[46]

It is not to our purpose to examine the other numerous Germanic codes from the fifth to the eighth centuries. The pattern is plain. To a greater or lesser extent each subsequent codification shows borrowing from Roman law and often from Visigothic law. The borrowings by the Germanic tribes were not always of the same rules, or to the same extent.

Rather it is appropriate to look briefly at the spread of Visigothic law within Spain, and first from the perspective of an old problem and a more recent, authoritative, rhetorical question. The old problem was the apparent profound Germanization of Spanish customary law in the High Middle Ages. The theory, developed principally by Ficker and Hinojosa, and widely supported, started from the observation that there was an intimate relationship between some High Medieval institutions in Spain and the corresponding Germanic ones in Norway and Iceland. These, it was argued, derived from a common ethnic Germanic source; hence there must have been a continued presence of Visigothic, that is Germanic, customary law in Spain from the eighth to the twelfth centuries along with and beneath the "legal law." In other words, because the Visigothic "legal law" was so Romanized and was in opposition to the customary law, its force in practice was limited and in many cases did not apply. The theory is not now considered acceptable[47] and in itself need not detain us here, but it did give rise to the important rhetorical question of the distinguished legal historian F. Tomás y Valiente: "Is it possible, historically and humanly speaking, that foreign and tiny minorities—though certainly dominant—who were extremely localized, and who lost their language, their culture, and their religion, could show themselves so terrifically expansive in the field of law, right to the point of imposing a profound Germanization on it?"[48] The Visigoths numbered somewhere between 80,000 and 200,000, less than 5 percent of the population of Spain, and they were in the main peasants settled around Toledo. Tomás y Valiente's question was obviously intended, as he goes on to suggest, to illicit a massive response in the negative. The question raises issues of fundamental importance for the growth and borrowing of law, but for us the focus of the question should be changed from the Visigoths' imposition of their customary law to their imposition—if that term can be applied to a voluntary acceptance—of their *Liber iudiciorum*. For, as is well known and as we shall see, the *Liber iudiciorum* came to prevail as the main law of Christian Spain. The obvious glib answer should be discarded. The more one might be tempted to say that the *Liber iudiciorum* could easily be accepted by the Hispano-Roman population because it was so Romanized, the more difficult becomes the issue of why the Visigoths, with a legal system based on Germanic custom, could borrow all that Roman law in the first place. And, of course, it should not be forgotten that the *Liber iudiciorum* contains much that is not Roman.

"With the exception of Justinian's legislation, this seventh-century Visigothic lawbook has enjoyed a wider authority during a longer time than any other code of secular law."[49] The Visigothic era in Spain ended in 711 as a result of the Moorish invasion, but the *Liber iudiciorum* did not vanish from sight. Law was, of course, much localized, and customary law remained powerful. With time, in those territories and for those people to whom the *Liber iudiciorum* applied, it either had its force and scope of application reduced or it had them increased.[50]

In Septimania and Catalonia, the *Liber iudiciorum* continued in force as the personal law of the *hispani*. Pipin declared in 769 that the inhabitants of Aquitania should live according to their personal law, and this was confirmed for all the *hispani* of Septimania and Catalonia by subsequent Carolingian rulers in a number of capitularies: this personal law was Visigothic law. The capitularies did also weaken the applicability of the *Liber iudiciorum*, because they settled questions of political order, military service, and criminal law, but the materials of the *Liber iudiciorum* were much used for private law. It was the most widely used law in Catalonia in the eighth to the tenth centuries. But it did decay with the growth of other local law. The local charters given to recovered territory had precedence over the *Liber iudiciorum*. Count Ramón Berenguer (1035–76) promulgated usages (*usatges*) to supplement the *Liber iudiciorum*, above all with regard to feudalization. In contracts there were frequent renunciations of the *Liber iudiciorum*, and in 1251 the Catalan Cortes forbade its invocation. The Mozarabs—that is, Christians living under Moorish rule—received the *Liber iudiciorum* as their personal law, and they retained it whether they fled into Christian kingdoms as a result of the persecution in the second half of the ninth century or whether the place in which they lived was reconquered. Elsewhere, throughout the Peninsula, there are also signs that the *Liber iudiciorum* was used: in Asturias, Galicia, northern Portugal, Navarre, and Aragon. But the deepest penetration was in Leon, where, from the tenth century, it was customary to decide lawsuits by its rules. Local *fueros* prevented it from having general force during the eleventh and twelfth centuries, but afterwards, until the reign of Alfonso IX, it was used as the law in force to cut down on appeal the judgments in the king's court and became ever more the general law of the kingdom. A similar happening occurred in Toledo.

None of the above is to be taken as suggesting that the acceptance of the *Liber iudiciorum* was anywhere complete. What was borrowed was not everywhere the same and was not everywhere to the same extent. What matters to us, though, is simply the fact that its contents were accepted in a greater or lesser degree as the law throughout the Peninsula, centuries after its promulgation, by peoples differing in many respects from the Visigoths. And its history does not stop with Alfonso IX. Ferdinand III of Castile (1230–52), the son of Alfonso IX, had the *Liber iudiciorum* officially translated into Castilian with the title of *Fuero Juzgo*. The *Fuero Juzgo* was then given, as if it were the local, individual *fuero*, to the towns as they were reconquered from the Moors: for instance, to Cordobá (1241), Cartagena (1243), Seville (1248). His son, Alfonso X (1252–84) gave the *Fuero Juzgo* as the local *fuero* on an even grander scale: to Alicante, Elche, Lorca, Murcia, and Talavera, for example. Subsequent kings continued the process. We need not pursue the matter further, for instance to note the spread of the *Fuero Juzgo* as part of the law of Castile to the New World.

Some Problem

After considering the growth of legal institutions, rules and ideas and the nature of customary law, and after looking at two major examples of legal borrowings, we are in a position to turn to the real issue of this chapter, the cause of the Reception of Roman law in Western Europe which began in the eleventh century, traditionally in Bologna with the teaching of the *Corpus Juris Civilis*, by Irnerius.[51] The cause of this Reception, you will recall, was described by Paul Vinogradoff as the most momentous and puzzling problem within the whole range of history. And the heading of this section of the chapter should be understood as a Glaswegian Scot would say, "*Some* problem, nae problem." The most momentous and puzzling problem within the whole range of history turns out to be a nonproblem!

The first part of this chapter and also the earlier chapters showed, I think, that legal development is to some considerable extent distinct from other developments in the society and in large measure is dictated by the tradition, relating to the law, that prevails among the legal elite. Law is by no means a perfect fit for the society, not even for the society in which and for which it is created. But in addition, the borrowing of another's law is a very potent means of legal growth. Even societies governed by custom frequently borrow much law from elsewhere, and customary legal systems may even be particularly susceptible to borrowing. I put it no stronger only because developed legal systems also borrow an enormous amount,[52] and I know of no way to measure the extent of borrowing. But on a priori grounds it makes sense to think that given the lack of law, especially clear law in customary legal systems, the relative lack of expertise in judges, and the common psychological need for authority in establishing legal rules,[53] the desire for borrowing would be relatively greater in customary systems.

The second part of the chapter was then mainly concerned with two major instances of massive legal borrowing: of much pre-Justinianic law by Germanic tribes from the fifth century onwards and of Visigothic law by Spanish peoples. These two instances give concreteness to the issues raised in the first part. Legal rules are not a perfect fit in the society for which they were created; absence of perfect fit, psychologically or economically, in a society which might borrow the law equally will be no obstacle to adoption. Massive borrowing is not total borrowing. Some legal institutions and rules will be borrowed entire, some with modifications that may be major; some will be replaced; some will be ignored entirely. A massive borrowing may continue over a long span of time. But the Reception of Roman law in the Germanic codes and of Visigothic law in Spain show much more than this. First, and above all, they show that (when the conditions are right) a great deal of law from a system constructed on very different lines or containing very different rules may be borrowed. Secondly, they—and above all the Germanic codes—show that a great deal of law can be borrowed from a society in which very different political, social, economic, and religious conditions prevail. Thirdly, they show the tendency, which is natural enough, to borrow from the more developed and detailed system. The cause of borrowing is often the search for a better rule, but it may be no more than the search for an established rule. Let us postulate in the latter case the borrowing of an apparently neutral rule. Let us suppose, as may have been true though we do not know, that the Burgundians previously had no fixed age for the attainment of majority or for the capacity to make a will. Let us further suppose that they have no firm opinions on the matter but the time has come for it to be useful to fix such ages. Nothing much, let us also suppose, turns upon the exact choice. So they choose the Roman ages of twenty-five and fourteen, respectively. Is that all there is to the matter? Not quite, I think. To begin with, the habit is being established of borrowing from one particular system whenever the rule there is not obviously inappropriate. Again, law develops ever more by analogy and by further borrowing. Other gaps in the law relating to majority or minority or capacity to make a will will require to be filled, and harmoniously they ought now to be filled for the Burgundians from Roman law. Fourthly, our two instances of borrowing show (what is amply documented in other instances) that law that is in writing, hence readily accessible, is *an* or *the* obvious source for borrowing: the success of the *Sachsenspiegel* in medieval Germany,[54] of the French *Code Civil* in Europe and Latin America,[55] of Blackstone's *Commentaries* in North America, are other powerful examples.[56] Points three and four lead on to a hypothesis. If Justinian's *Corpus Juris Civilis*, especially his *Code*, had been known in Spain at the time of the reception of the Visigothic Code, as we know that it was not,[57] then it would have been a formidable rival to the *Visigothic Code*. It would have had all the right credentials: it was in writing, hence accessible (if known), and was more sophisticated and detailed than the law of the possible borrowers. In addition, it had a further, attractive, but not necessary, quality as a prospective quarry: like the *Visigothic Code* its contents, as a result of previous transplanting, had much in common with the law of the possible borrowers. The Hispano-Romans had pre-Justinianic Roman law as their law even if largely drawn from Roman vulgar law; the *Corpus Juris Civilis* contained much of the preceding Roman law. Similarly, the *Visigothic Code*, containing much Roman and Germanic law, had a great deal in common with the law of the *hispani*.

Imagine then the situation of one detailed, massive, advanced system of law in writing coming within the orbit of a number of legal systems, each involving a relatively small number of persons (hence with limitations on the amount of original legal talent available), each primarily a customary system with regard to the legal institutions dealt with by the system in writing; imagine also no intense hostility—for instance, on religious grounds—towards the culture whose legal system was in writing. In such circumstances it would be inconceivable, even if the system in writing arose from a very different society, that the customary systems would not, one by one, each within its own time frame and for its own purposes and to varying extents, begin to borrow legal rules, approaches, and ideas. What was borrowed for one customary system would not necessarily be the same as what was borrowed for another, but the process of borrowing would continue, each borrowing suggesting the appropriateness of another borrowing.

A further factor should be thrown into the equation. It seems reasonable to think, even if it cannot always be proved, that when one legal system is habitually chosen as the source from which to borrow, then that system is regarded as having high quality.[58] I know of no evidence, other than circumstantial, to indicate that the Germans of the fifth and immediately following centuries had such an opinion of Roman law, or that inhabitants of Spain at the time of the reconquest felt that way about the *Visigothic Code*. But there is direct evidence of enormous respect for Roman law on the eve of the Reception. In the Frankish empire there were numerous "capitularies," in the sense of royal legislation. One distinct type, *capitula legibus addenda*, "capitularies to be added to laws," were issued in order to supplement or amend existing law, and they might be added to a particular lawbook such as the *Lex Saxonum, Lex Salica, Lex Baiuwariorum,* and so on. But in the Frankish empire Roman law was also personal law. And, as has been pointed out,[59] it is remarkable that no capitularies supplementing Roman law have been found. King Carolus II in a capitulary of A.D. 864 modifying existing law expressly excludes its operation on Roman law: "But in these places where lawsuits are judged according to Roman law, let those persons committing such acts be judged in accordance with that law: because neither did our predecessors issue any capitulary nor do we lay down anything to supplement that law or against that law."[60] The reason is plain: no one could imagine Roman law to be capable of improvement. And at this time the *Corpus Juris Civilis* was not known!

Nothing more need be said. The cause of the Reception of Roman law is sufficiently explained. Other causes might be adduced, and ought to be adduced in the right place, to explain why it began where it did, and when it did, and why it took the particular forms that it did. But to deal with these here would only complicate and confuse the issue. The task here is finished once it is demonstrated that the most momentous and puzzling problem of history is no problem, that it corresponds to the cultural norms of massive, voluntary legal borrowing, and that it is a non-Reception which would have constituted the most puzzling problem of history. The first (and most) important step in understanding the Reception is to know that we should explain its cause by not explaining its causes.

IV

Evolution and Revolution

Evolution

The main themes of the three preceding chapters can all be pulled together if one looks at medieval or Renaissance case law. I have chosen to use only one not atypical example from seventeenth-century Scotland. It is the pleading of Sir George Mackenzie (born 1636, died 1691) before the Supreme Court of Scotland for the defender Haining, which also quotes the arguments for the pursuers, the fishers upon Tweed.[1] Advocates' speeches of the period are much fuller than are the reports of the judicial decisions. In Mackenzie's collected works this is the first pleading on Scots law.

Scots private law in the seventeenth century was custom or consuetude when there was not (as there often was not) a statute.[2] Judicial decision was also very pertinent. Stair, in the second edition of his *Institutions of the Law of Scotland* (1.1.16), seems in fact to regard a number of decisions as forming a custom.[3] Thus, Scots law of the time can properly be regarded as a mature system of law which was largely customary. For both Stair and Mackenzie, in the absence of local custom, canon law and especially civil law carried great weight because of their high quality.[4]

Mackenzie's pleading runs as follows:

For
HAINING
Against
The Fishers upon Tweed.

How far a Man may use his own, tho' to the Prejudice of his Neighbours?

Haining being prejudged by a Lake which overflow'd his Ground, and which by its Nearness to his House, did, as is ordinary for standing Waters, impair very much the Health of his Family: He did therefore open the said Lake, whose Waters being received by *Whittater*, did at last run with *Whittater* into *Tweed*. The Fishers upon that River, pretending that the Water which came from that Lake did kill their Salmond [*sic*], and occasion their leaving the River, do crave that *Haining* may be ordain'd to close up that Passage. This being the State of the Case, it was alledged for *Haining*.

That since Men had receded from that first Community, which seem'd to be establish'd amongst them by Nature, the Law made it its great Task, to secure every Man in the free and absolute Exercise of his Property, and did allow him to use his own as he thought fit, and whatever did lessen this Power and Liberty, is by the common Law term'd a Servitude, or Slavery; nor can a Servitude be imposed upon a Man without his own Consent. And suitably to this Principle, every Man may raise his own House as high as he pleases, tho' he should thereby obscure the Lights of his Neighbour's House: Or if I should abstract from my Neighbour's Ponds, that Water which formerly run into them from my Lands, the Law doth not think him prejudged, nor me obliged to prefer his Conveniency to my own Inclinations, as is clear by *1.26.ff de damno infect*. For as that Law very well observes, he is not prejudged who loses a Benefit, which flow'd from him who was no Way ty'd to bestow it, *1.26.ff. de dam. infect*. Proculus ait, *Cum quis jure quid in suo faceret quamvis promisisset damni infecti vicino, non tamen eum teneri ea stipulatione: Veluti si juxta mea aedificia habeas aedificia eaque jure tuo altius tollas, aut si in vicino tuo agro cuniculo, vel fossa aquam meam avoces. Quamvis enim & hic aquam mihi abducas, & illic luminibus officias, tamen ex ea stipulatione actionem mihi non competere: scil. quia non debeat videri is damnum facere, qui eo veluti lucro quo adhuc utebatur, prohibetur: Multumque interesse utrum damnum quis faciat, an lucro, quod adhuc faciebat, uti prohibeatur.* And if I dig a Well in my own House, which may cut off those Passages whereby Water was conveyed to my Neighbour's Well, one of the greatest Lawyers has upon this Case resolved, that my Neighbour will not prevail against me; *For,* saith he, *no Man can be said to be wrong'd by what I do upon my own Ground, for in this I use my own Right, 1.24. §12. ff eod. In domo mea puteum aperio quo aperto venae putei tui praecisae sunt, an tenear? Ait* Trebatius, *Me non teneri damni infecti, neque enim existimari operis mei vitio damnum tibi dari, in ea re, in qua jure meo usus sum:* Where the Gloss observes, that *in suo quod quisque fecerit, in damnum vicini id non animo nocendi facere presumitur.* And if by a Wall or Fence upon my Land, the Water was kept from overflowing my Neighbour's Land, I may throw down my own Fence, tho' my Neighbour's Land be thereby overflowed, *1. 21. ff. de aqua pluvia.* And therefore, seeing the Ground doth belong to *Haining,* and that the Fishers of *Tweed* have no Servitude upon him, he may use his own as he pleases, especially seeing he doth not immediately send his Water into *Tweed,* but into another Rivulet, which carries it very far before it doth disgorge there. So that if the Fishers upon *Tweed* did prevail against *Haining,* they might likewise prevail against all from whose Ground any Moss-water runs into *Tweed,* tho' at Fifty Miles Distance; and they may forbid all the Towns from which any Water runs into *Tweed,* to throw in any Excrements, or any Water employ'd in Dying, lest it prejudge their Salmon-fishing; whereas, *Alteri prodesse, ad liberalitatem, non ad justitiam pertinent* [sic].

It is (My Lords) referr'd to your Consideration, that public Rivers have been very wisely by Providence, spread up and down the World, to be easie, and natural Vehicles for conveying away to the Sea, (that great Receptacle of all Things that are unnecessary) Excrements, and other noxious Things, which would otherwise have very much prejudged Mankind; and that they may the better perform this Office, Providence has bestow'd upon Rivers a purifying and cleansing Quality, so that after a little Time, and a very short Course, all that is thrown in there, doth happily lose their noxious Nature, which is wash'd off by the Streams by which they are carried.

Rivers are Nature's High-ways by Water, and we may as well forbid to carry any Thing that smells ill, upon our High-ways by Land, as we may forbid to throw in stinking Waters into our Rivers. The proper Use of Rivers is, that they should be portable, and fit for

Navigation, or for transporting Things from one Place into another; and Salmon-fishing is but an accidental Casuality, and therefore the only Interdicts or Prohibitions propon'd by the Law, relating to public Rivers are, *Ne quid in flumine ripave ejus fiat, quo pejus navigetur, tit. 12 lib. 53.* and, *ut in flumine publico navigare liceat, tit. 14. ff. eod. lib.* But in Rivers that are not navigable, the Law has forbidden nothing, but that their Course and natural Current be not alter'd, *Ne quid in flumine publico fiat, quo aliter fluat aqua, atque uti priore estate fluxit, tit. 13. ibidem.* So that since the Law doth not forbid the throwing in any Thing into public Rivers, it doth allow it; for it is free for every Man to do what the Law hath not prohibited: And if upon such capricious Suggestions as these, Men were to be restrain'd from using their own, no Man should ever adventure to drain his Land, to open Coal-sinks, or Lead-mines, or to seek out any Minerals whatsoever, whose Waters are of all other the most pestilentious, because after he had bestow'd a great deal of Expence, he might be forc'd to desist, for satisfying the Jealousy, or Imagination of melancholy or avaritious Neighbours. And if this Pursuit find a favourable Hearing, Malice and Envy will make use of it, as a fair Occasion whereby to disturb all successful and thriving Undertakers. But your Lordships may see, that the World, both learn'd and unlearn'd, have hitherto believ'd, that such a Pursuit as this would not be sustain'd, in that tho' Interest and Malice did prompt Men to such Pursuits, yet no one such as this has ever been intented, for ought I could ever read, save once at *Grenoble,* where an Advocate did pursue a Smith to transport his Forge from the chief Street, because it did by its Noise disturb not only him, but the People who frequented that Street; from which Pursuit the Smith was absolved, as *Expilly* observes in his Pleading.

Yet, my Lords, the Fishers upon *Tweed* want not some apparent Reasons which give Colour to the Pursuit; and it is urg'd for them, "That no Man is so Master of his own, but that the Commonwealth has still an Interest with him in it; and Law being invented to protect the Interest of Societies, as well as to secure the Property of private Persons: Therefore tho' every private Man inclines to satisfy his own Humour and Advantage, in the Use of what is his own; yet it is the Interest of the Commonwealth, that he do not abuse his own Property; and therefore it is, that the Law doth interdict Prodigals; nor will the Law suffer that a Man use his own *in emulationem alterius, 1. 3. ff. de oper. pub.* and a Man is said to do any Thing *in emulationem alterius,* when others lose more by what is done, than the

Proprietar can gain: As in this Case, tho' *quilibet potest facere in suo*, yet *non potest immittere in alienum*, which is their Case; and all the Arguments brought for *Haining* do not meet, seeing they only prove, that a Man may use what is his own as he pleases, *ubi nihil immittit in alienum*; as is clear by the Instances given, of throwing down his own Wall, or the digging up a Well in his own Land, which differs very much from our Case, wherein *Haining* doth pour in his poysonous Water into the River of *Tweed*.

That Men are restrain'd for the Good of the Commonwealth in the Use of their own Property, is very clear from many Instances in our Law, as Men are discharg'd by Acts of Parliament to burn Moors, to kill Smolts; the Way and Manner of Fishing upon *Lochleven* is prescribed to the Heritors by Act of Parliament, and Men are forbidden to steep Lint by public Acts likewise. Likeas, the common Law will not suffer Men so to use Water running thro' their own Land, as that they may thereby prejudge Mills belonging to their Neighbours, which use to go by that Water: And whatever may be alledged in favour of any Innovation in running Waters; yet Lakes being appointed by Nature, seem to have from Nature a fix'd Being; nor should they be open'd to the Prejudice of others, contrary to their Nature."

These Objections may (my Lords) be thus satisfied. To the First, it is answered, That the only Two Restrictions put upon Men in the free Exercise of their own, are, *ne in alterius emulationem fiat, vel materiam seditionis praebeat*, as is clear by the foresaid *1.3. ff. de oper. pub.* neither of which can be subsumed in this Case. And when the Law considers what is done *in emulationem alterius*, it acknowledges, *illud non factum esse in emulationem alterius, quod factum est principaliter ut agenti profit, & non ut alteri noceat, 1. fluminum § fin. ff. de dam. infect.* and the Gloss formerly cited upon that Law determines, that *Animus nocendi* is not presum'd, if any other Cause can be assigned: And in this Case, *Haining* can ascribe his opening this Lake to the Prejudice it did to his Land, and to his Health; whereas it cannot be alledged, that he ever express'd any Malice against the Fishers upon *Tweed*, many of whom are his own Relations. As to the Instances given, wherein the Law doth restrict the free Use of Property, the Principle is not deny'd but it is misapply'd. For the Law only bounds the Proprietar's Power in some Cases, wherein his Loss may be otherwise supply'd; as in Moor-burn, and killing of Smolts at such a Season of the Year, and in steeping Lint in running Waters, which may be as commodiously done in standing Pools; but these Pursuers crave this Lake to be stopt at all Times. Nor is there an apparent Reason here as there, this Pursuit being founded only upon a conjectural Prejudice; and in these Cases, the Prohibition is made necessary by the Generality and Frequency of Occurrences, and yet tho' so circumstantiated, there is still a public Law necessary. And when a public Law discharges the free Exercise of Property, it ordains him in whose Favours the Prohibition is, to refound his Expences who is prohibited. Nor is the Commonwealth here prejudg'd so much by this, as it would be by the contrary; for thereby all Coal-heughs, Lead-mines, and the winning of other Minerals would be discharg'd: Whereas it is uncertain if this Water chaseth away the Salmon, which are at best but a Casuality, and which will go but from *Tweed* to other Rivers in *Scotland;* for they cannot stay in the Sea. Salmon-fishing is but an Accident to Rivers, but these being the common Porters is their natural Use. Thus (my Lords) you see that we contend for what is natural to Rivers; they for what is but casual; we are founded upon the Nature and Privilege of Property, they upon mere Conjectures.

THE *Lords enclin'd to sustain Haining's*
Defence; but, before Answer, they granted
Commission for examining upon the Place,
what Prejudice was done.

If we restrict our gaze only to the law and legal argument, the first thing to be noticed in the case is that on this relatively large issue—especially as expressed at the outset as the legal question to be answered—there is a complete gap in the law. No Scottish statute or legal decision is cited for the general issue of how far one may use one's own property although another is injured. The same holds true for another question: how far may one, for one's own benefit, cause deterioration in the quality of flowing water. As often in a customary system, there is no established law, and also there is no way—or at least no way is sought—to determine what practice is followed as a norm. So Mackenzie moves straight to the citation of Roman law. He offers no justification for this, even though Roman law was no binding authority. But it is, first of all, the admired system; secondly, it is an accessible system in writing, and much fuller in detail than Scots law; thirdly, the tradition among advocates and judges has been to turn to this system; and fourthly, Scots law has already filled gaps from Roman law, thus making further borrowing seem harmonious. We can appreciate how natural it becomes to develop law in this way.

But something that may appear vital is missing in this appeal to Roman law for the filling of gaps, namely societal concerns or the relationship of law to society. With respect specifically to the free use of public rivers, Mackenize seeks of Roman law only knowledge of the remedies given for interference with their use. And he finds interdicts relating to hindering or preventing navigation, and with regard to rivers that need not be navigable only a legal prohibition against changing their course. But he does not then ask whether the societal interests of the ancient Romans were the same as those of the contemporary Scots. Whatever answer we might want to give, it is surely significant that neither he nor his adversary apparently thought fit to include the question and an answer in their pleadings. And the fact is that in Scotland there were important societal rights in a river that had no counterpart in Italy, precisely the societal rights adversely affected by Haining's behavior, salmon fishing. And these societal rights were governed by law long before the time of Mackenzie.

Legislation on salmon fishing—and remember, legislation was relatively uncommon—existed as early as the thirteenth century, and there was much subsequent legislation.[6] And salmon fishing was distinguished in law from the fishing for all other river fish.[7] It was indeed a royal right, though different from all other royal rights. The details need not detain us here, but Baron David Hume in his lectures (1786–1822) could say:

But, as to all the higher and more profitable modes of fishing for salmon, with long net and coble—or with currachs, —or by cruives, and standing nets, —and in short the different whole-sale ways of taking them—the right is a Royal right—and which none of the lieges, heritor or not, can exercise on a proper public river—or any river, that is large enough to afford those profitable modes of fishing, —without a grant and title from the Crown.[8]

Such a grant from the Crown was held by the fishers upon Tweed. The point I wish to make is that if, in the absence of pertinent Scots law, discussion of legal problems had centered on what legal rules would be best for Scottish societal conditions, and not—as was dictated by the legal tradition—on what were the Roman legal rules and the principles behind them, then the thrust of the debate, and possibly the result of the trial, would have been different.

We have not finished with Mackenzie's defense, but now we should consider the pursuers' case. A man, they say, cannot use his own property just as he likes: society also has an interest. Hence he cannot abuse his property, and it is for this reason that prodigals are interdicted. Scotland had long known the interdiction of prodigals,[9] a notion probably itself derived from Roman law. The argument is not a strong one, and is not insisted on. The second point is expressed in Roman law terms—one must not deal with one's property *in emulationem alterius*—with a Roman law citation. But the law is wrongly stated, both for Rome and Scotland.[10] Neither country accepted the notion that one so acted when the loss to others was greater than the possible gain to oneself. In both, the decisive issue was the intention. The pursuers had no real argument here, which might explain why they cite no authority from Scots law. Mackenzie, be it noted, correctly rebuts the argument, and he likewise cites no Scots law.

The next argument is apparently in rebuttal of an argument for Haining: one may use one's own as one pleases only *ubi nihil immitit in alienum,* when one does not send something onto another's property. And Haining, the pursuers claim, poured his poisonous water into the Tweed. Two separate legal points may be involved here, and Mackenzie certainly refers to both of them. The first seems to turn on the issue of a servitude, with the pursuers claiming they were not subject to one. As Stair puts it, "What hath been said of stillicides, holdeth more apparently in sinks either for conveying of water, filth, or any thing else, upon or through the neighbour's tenements, which cannot be done, unless there be a servitude thereupon either by consent or prescription."[11] But the requirement of a servitude to send water through another's property applied only to towns. In the country, one could let water drain onto or through a neighbor's land with impunity.[12] Mackenzie turns the argument around: Haining can send his loch water into the rivers, because he is not bound by any servitude to the fishers of Tweed. And, of course, he could not be, since a servitude existed only over bounding property.

The second legal point is perhaps ignored by the pursuers: at least it is not pressed with vigor. The Roman *actio aquae pluviae arcendae* gave a remedy where, as a result of human activity, water resulting from rain would flow onto another's land and cause loss. The Roman action was worked out in great detail: not every human activity would give rise to the action, since certain kinds of agricultural work were exempt from liability,[13] and what counted as rainwater was much disputed. But for the present case, draining the loch would not be an exempt activity; loch water would be rainwater; and the action was available in the country (but not in towns). The Roman action was intended primarily to have the defendant prevent future damage by the water,[14] and this is precisely what the fishers of Tweed demanded. The point where difficulties might arise for the pursuers is that the Roman texts are concerned with resulting injuries on another's land, not in the water itself. But an extension might have been argued for. From this distance one might think that the *actio aquae pluviae arcendae* would have given the pursuers their best legal argument, but the fact is that neither the action nor an equivalent was prominent in Scots law. It does not appear in Stair or Mackenzie.

Very instructive is the treatment a century and a half later by
Baron Hume in his lectures:

With this rule coincides that precept of the *Roman* Law (and observed in ours), *"ne immittas in alienum,"* that one shall not send,
throw or direct any thing, such for instance as a stream of water,
into the property of one's neighbour, to harm him. The operation,
it is true, commences *in suo,* within the bounds of one's own ten-
ement; but it has an instant, an intended, and a foreseen, a necessary continuation into the next one and is much the same in substance as the doing of something there. Take the case of one who
has a lake, or loch in his grounds and who wishes to drain the loch.
Now here, if there be no natural runner into which to conduct the
water, he is not at liberty to open a vent for it through his march,
leaving it to his neighbour to rid himself of the water as he best
may. He must buy the necessary level or channel from his neighbour, who may refuse to deal with him if he please; and, when
bought, it must be scoured and kept in condition for its uses, and
at his own expense. I refer you on that head to the case of *Gray* v.
Maxwell, 30 July 1762 (Kaimes).[15]

He begins as if discussing the servitude already mentioned, but
then goes on as if he is treating of the *actio aquae pluviae arcendae.*
He allows it, though the circumstances he relates are significantly
different from Haining's case. And a few pages further on he
seems to express a different view:

Last of all, as to water collected in a Loch or Lake, which is a subject of a different condition from a stream. If a lake be encompassed
by the lands of one heritor only, and there be no sort of stream or
discharge from it, certainly he is owner of the lake, as much as of
the lands, and may drain or dispose of it at his pleasure, if he have
the means of carrying off the water through his own lands. This, I
say, holds in his favor unless, by usage of watering, or otherwise,
his neighbours have established a servitude of some sort, to restrain
him.[16]

The obvious conclusion to be drawn is that even by this time the
actio aquae pluviae arcendae had not become well-established in

Scotland. Even much later in the century it was still very questionable whether draining a lake so that the flow of water was hurtful to lower ground gave rise to an action.[17] The reason for this is obscure: the utility of the *actio aquae pluviae arcendae* had been known to the Romans as early as the fifth century B.C. Perhaps the difference in climatic conditions is relevant: the need for proper drainage of higher land would be more apparent in Scotland,[18] and since rain there falls less torrentially than in Italy, lower-lying proprietors would be affected less dramatically. But this explanation does not seem too persuasive. The Scots also failed to adopt to any extent the related Roman remedies for *damnum infectum*, future loss, which would have been as useful in one country as in the other. In any event, the interest of the matter for us is that a borrower need not take all its law from the prime outside authoritative source, and a failure to borrow may at times be as difficult to explain on societal terms as borrowing can be.

Mackenzie makes the point that if there were restraints on polluting rivers, the working of coal-pits and lead mines would be inhibited, and that these are more valuable to the society than salmon fishing. Quite so, and the Romans were as aware as the Scots of the pestilential effluvia of lead and silver mines, and such workings were at least as economically valuable to the Romans. But the important societal difference between Scotland and Rome was precisely that the rights of salmon fishing in the former but not the latter were economically valuable and in this regard were left unprotected.[19] The growth of law in Scotland restraining the pollution of water was, in fact, slow. The earliest case in which an interdict was granted against polluting a stream was decided in 1791, and the owners of salmon fisheries were being protected by 1886.[20] It took until fairly late in the nineteenth century for it to be well-established that a stream was not to be polluted "so as to be made unfit for the use of man or beast."[21]

None of the legal arguments adduced on either side, apart perhaps from that of Mackenzie just discussed, rely on local societal conditions. Rather they show the importance of the legal tradition. One final argument of Mackenzie is rooted in the legal tradition and is independent of place but not of time. He contends, he says, for what is natural, the other side for what is only casual. The reference to the Law of Nature of this type is to be expected only in the Age of Reason.[22]

Many thousands of cases, from all over Western Europe from the twelfth century at the latest onwards, could be chosen to illustrate the same points. But any choice of examples would of necessity be arbitrary, nothing is gained by offering a few more cases, and this one case may stand for all, exemplifying both success and failure of legal development and of legal borrowing.[23]

The main conclusion that I think ought to be drawn from this chapter is the converse of all that has gone before. No case of Haining's type—and, I venture to believe, no case at all—can be fully understood as an instance of law in action unless one takes into account the thrust of the preceding chapters: that the legal tradition sets the parameters of the debate, that customary law may well not emerge from local normative practices, and that some "foreign" legal system may be so admired in general by the lawyers that they are dazzled, and at least half-blinded to local concerns. Not all cases are affected by such factors to the same extent—some cases do not concern customary law; in some the impact of law from another time and place is much in the background (though scarcely ever entirely absent)—but none is ever independent.

Revolution

To all of what has been said in this and the previous chapters a possible objection might be raised. What, it might be asked, about revolution in law? It seems that there can be sudden drastic change in law: the introduction of the French *Code Civil* for instance, or its acceptance in some South American state, or the approach to law in Russia after the Socialist Revolution or

Ataturk's legal reforms. How does sudden massive legal change affect the picture of legal development that has been presented? The answer, I believe, is that an examination of revolution in law confirms the general thesis of the enormous impact of the legal tradition on legal change.

Revolutions in law occur, I believe, in four sets of circumstances which, it should be emphasized, shade into one another. First, where the law has, largely through the impact of the legal tradition, become cumbrous and remote from societal realities, and there is a profound call for improvement. Secondly, where the realistic possibility is presented of borrowing a foreign system in large measure. Thirdly, where there has been an actual political revolution, and societal conditions have changed. Fourthly where the ruling elite wishes to change society drastically, to revolutionize society, and chooses to use law as one tool. These four sets of circumstances will be discussed in order.

For the first case, the best examples are, I believe, to be sought in some modern codes such as the *Codex Maximilianeus Bavaricus civilis* of Bavaria (1756), the Prussian *Allgemeines Landrecht für die Preussischen Staaten* (1794) and the Austrian *Allgemeines Bürgerliches Gesetzbuch* (1812). But they are all, as legal historians know, deeply rooted in the preceding legal tradition.[24] The concern of the lawmakers was much more to make the law more comprehensible and accessible than to change drastically the legal rules.[25] The formulation of these codes represents a decisive stage in the development of the law of their territory: from now on the authority of the territorial law is to rest primarily on statute rather than on custom and the *Corpus Juris Civilis*. Most of what could usefully be borrowed from the *Corpus Juris* has been. There is a turning toward new sources of legal growth but no rejection of the existing heritage of legal rules. Two contemporary private initiatives for a code for all Germany are revealing of attitudes, as even the titles of their work shows. In 1777 Johann Georg Schlosser published his *Vorschlag und Versuch einer Verbesserung des deutschen bürgerlichen Rechts ohne Ab-*

schaffung des römischen Gesetzbuchs (Recommendation and attempt at an improvement of German civil law without the abrogation of the Roman code). And in 1800 came Johann Friedrich Reitemeier's *Ueber die Redaction eines Deutschen Gesetzbuchs aus den brauchbaren aber unveränderten Materialien des gemeinen Rechts in Deutschland* (On the redaction of a German code from the usable but unchanged materials of the common law in Germany). The Bavarian Code, too, had kept the previous law as law in force. That could not be the way forward. But nonetheless, such books and that code indicate there was to be no break with the legal tradition. The draftsmen of the codes were not seeking a new set of very different legal rules, but the same or very similar rules, with modifications, made clearer, simpler, and less controverted. Acceptance of a code does require official, political intervention, but history shows that codification can occur under any type of government.[26]

For the second case, the best examples are to be found in the wholesale adoption of the French civil code as a model for a civil code in Latin American countries and in parts of Europe.[27] Here, too, it was the legal tradition that dictated the changes. The borrowing nations might have had a very different economy or political structure from France at the time of Napoleon. What they had in common were a system of law similar to that of France before codification, a civil law system which accepted the authority of the *Corpus Juris*,[28] and a desire to set out the law in a more accessible form. They did not necessarily want to create a society like that of France. For those imbued with this legal tradition the French *Code Civil* was often the most obvious, if not the only, model. Significantly, no country without a civil law tradition followed this path.

For the third case, the obvious examples should be chosen from the French Revolution and the Soviet Revolution. Here again we should remember that a legal institution is a social institution looked at from the legal point of view. If the social institution disappears, then so should the legal institution (though it may leave traces); if a new social institution emerges, then it is likely to be surrounded by applicable legal rules. The French Revolution destroyed the social institution of feudalism in France: with that destruction disappeared all the legal incidences of feudalism. But no one has, I believe, ever doubted that France remained, what she was before, a civil law country and, indeed, for many became the civil law country par excellence. However much society changed, the basic civilian approaches and rules remained.

The Soviet Revolution was much more drastic in its attempt to change both the basis of society and law. According to Marxist doctrine, law is only a superstructure: it is an instrument of those who exercise their dictatorship because they have under their control the instruments of production. Law in a capitalist state, for instance, is unjust, suppressing the interests of the exploited classes.[29] This attitude to law is therefore in strict contrast to the bourgeois notions of law which preceded it. If in such circumstances no trace remained of the preceding legal tradition, that would not be contrary to the thesis of this book. Naturally political will and political power have an impact on legal rules and the legal tradition; and here we would have an extreme case of political will using political power to change society, using law as one instrument of this change. Since the previous law and legal tradition were wicked, they, too, would have to change. One legal tradition would be replacing another. And in many regards Soviet law is very different from earlier Russian law. Yet when that is said, it must also be maintained that the preceding legal tradition has not relinquished its influence. Before the Revolution Russian law could be classed within the civil law family though it was not a full member.[30] Today, among Western jurists at any rate, the issue is still discussed whether Soviet law should be classed as a civil law system. For some there is no doubt that it should, even though stress is laid on the impact of Marxist-Leninist principles. E. L. Johnson puts it this way:

Soviet law, like Imperial Russian law (at any rate after 1864),
clearly falls within the civil law group of legal systems. This presents
particular problems for Anglo-American students of the Soviet system, whereas for the continental students, there is much, especially
in the way of principle and terminology, that a French or Dutch stu-
dent may be able to take for granted; he is, in effect, enabled to
concentrate on the differences between Soviet law and his own system, just by reason of the fact that certain basic assumptions and, in
particular, certain matters of terminology are similar. The French re-
search worker, for example, who finds some Soviet rule, institution,
or juridical technique that differs from his own, will usually want to
find out whether that particular rule, institution or technique was
paralleled in the Imperial Russian legal system, for only then can he
decide whether it is to be regarded as a specific feature of the Soviet
legal system or whether it is part of the Russian legal heritage ac-
quired and taken over, perhaps with modifications, by the Soviets.
In other words, he asks himself, does this rule or institution have a
specifically Soviet or a specifically Russian character? The Anglo-
American lawyer researching into Soviet law, however, who finds
some rule or institution of an unfamiliar nature, has first to pose a
preliminary question; is this rule or feature a common characteristic
of civil law systems in general, as distinct from common law
systems? Only when he is satisfied that it is not can he go on to
consider whether he is dealing with some specifically Russian or
specifically Soviet rule or institution.[31]

Others prefer to class socialist law as a separate family.[32] Among
them some stress that, outside of Russia, much of the old law was
retained in the socialist states: "Techniques known from experience to be valuable and which were in no way incompatible with
a renewal of the law were preserved. Substantively, legal provisions in which class characteristics were evident were abrogated; but the whole of the law was not condemned since it
contained a portion of the national cultural heritage that was
worthy of admiration and confidence."[33] Others emphasize even
for Russia the continued influence of German law in the Civil
Code of the RSFSR of 1922.[34] Prerevolutionary drafts of codes
were heavily based on German law. The RSFSR civil codes of

1922 and 1964 both have a "General Part" which corresponds closely in nature, intention, and contents to the "Allgemeiner Teil" of the German *Bürgerliches Gesetzbuch*, and both treat the specific types of contract in a manner very similar to that found in the *BGB*. This survival of the preceding legal tradition is deeply significant.

The fourth situation should be discussed for the sake of completeness, but here, I wonder what is to be learned for or against the impact of the legal tradition on legal development. In the extreme case, one legal tradition is to be replaced by a second, in order to change societal institutions. If the result is a total and immediate success for the transplant, we would know that (in particular circumstances) societal (and with them legal) institutions can be rapidly altered by the imposition of political will using law as one instrument of change. If the result is a total failure, we would know (in particular circumstances) societal (and with them legal) institutions cannot be rapidly altered by the imposition of the political will. This kind of case is very common, especially perhaps in countries which have just won their independence. In the absence of sustained political opposition, the result is a more or less slow acceptance of the new legal rules. The speed of transition depends on many facts, including education in the new tradition. Penetration is thus often slowest in villages, where there is least impact on daily living from the official law and more acceptance of the traditional law, where illiteracy, including that of legal officials, makes understanding of the new law difficult, and where established local procedures are often cheapest.[35]

What the four situations have in common, especially one, three, and four, is that they represent the legal tradition in crisis, when law is seen and treated most clearly as a means, not an end.[36] The force of the legal tradition is, in fact, threatened. The remarkable fact then is not that that occurs, but that when it does, the legal tradition retains so much of its authority and power. Theoretically at least the legal tradition may be entirely superseded. When it is, it is replaced by another legal tradition.

V

Conclusions

By the very fact of becoming law, ideas and claims of right come to exist in their own right as legal ideas and legal rules, and they form their own societal unit. To some extent they coincide, and perhaps ideally they ought entirely to coincide,[1] with other societal institutions and with the needs and desires either of the people forming the society or of the ruling elite. But those working with the law estimate the rules by their "lawness," by their being or not being law. Law has its own standard for existence. Law is a means to an end and cannot be an end in itself, but lawyers—however widely one may define that term—have an inherent tendency to look upon legal rules as if they were ends in themselves; for them a course of action is properly to be followed because it is in accordance with law, even if the reason for the law can no longer be discovered or if the society has changed and the legal rule is no longer appropriate.

Of all law, custom should most closely match society. Indeed, in its own sphere (that is, the sphere of law), it should be a mirror image. It is not imposed from above, arbitrarily perhaps, but, as the standard theory has it, is law because the people follow it as law, and it corresponds to their normative behavior and changes when the behavior changes. But all this is far from the truth. The truth is patent in the sources; it is noted by legal historians and anthropologists; yet the obvious conclusions are not drawn.

Those writing down their customs stress the antiquity of those customs, but the social mores may have changed. They stress the difficulty of finding the law, so how can it have emerged from normative behavior accepted by the people as law? They say at times that after strenuous effort they have found the custom in antique decisions and documents, so the problems raised by the issues just mentioned are compounded. Legal questions are continually asked to which there is no answer in the custom and for which there is no legal machinery to settle the scope of principles or rules. Standard methods develop to help fill gaps in the law, whether this is to choose other folks' custom as one's own subsidiary custom, or to treat another town as one's "mother" in legal matters and send there for a reply to a legal problem, or habitually to resort to the rules of another system. But whatever approach is adopted, the overwhelming tendency is to turn to a more developed legal system. Great disparity in legal structure or sophistication is no bar to borrowing. But the more complex law is likely to have been the product of a more developed economy: the Custom of Paris is looked to by small, rural southern French towns; the law of thriving Magdeburg, by remote Polish settlements; Roman law, by wandering German tribes. Not only is the borrowed law "foreign" law; it is also the law of economically and politically different cultures. Customary law is above all to be found in court decisions, and is discovered by the judges whether there was a custom or whether a "custom" was invented by the judge or, more likely, borrowed by the judge from elsewhere. Customary law when it is accepted as law is judge-made law, hence is subject to the influence of the legal tradition. As judge-made law it is, moreover, "official" law; customary law is law only insofar as it is acceptable to the rulers.

The extent to which legal rules in customary (and, indeed, other) systems do not fit the society particularly well and are even disfunctional is often concealed by a failure to distinguish clearly between the societal institution and the legal institution. A legal institution is a social institution which has been given legal effectiveness and which is being regarded from the legal point of view. Without the social institution of slavery there will be (in almost all cases at least) no legal institution of slavery. In a society exclusively of small peasant farmers there may be law for small peasant farms but not for high-rises. We have been told nothing about how well law functions in a society when we learn that it does not exist apart from its relevant social institution. That without peasant farms or high-rises there will be no law about peasant farms or high-rises does not entail the conclusion—apparently often assumed—that, because in a society there is law about peasant farms and there are peasant farms and there are no high-rises and no law about high-rises, the law is in congruence with the society.

When we turn to more developed law, we find the same phenomena. Society has its input, which may be vigorously expressed or be tacit but demonstrated by obvious needs, overwhelming or minor. The legal tradition shapes the law that comes out: divisions, classifications, types of remedy, scope of rules and exceptions, all matters of great practical consequence. As a result of societal pressure, say, the law has to be changed: the resulting law will usually be borrowed, from a system known to the legal elite, often with modifications, to be sure, but not always those deemed appropriate after full consideration of local conditions. The input of the society often bears little relation to the output of the legal elite. This remains true no matter what the principal sources of law are, though the relative impact of societal forces and the legal tradition on these varies from one source to another.[2]

Thus, the direct link between a society and its law is tenuous, whether the law is customary or formed by professional full-time lawyers. Legal development depends on the lawyers' culture. When an issue arises, whether in theory or in practice, and requires a legal answer, the lawyers habitually seek authority.

Hence it is that to an enormous extent law develops by borrowing from another place and even from another time. This may be after a systematic search for the best law, but typically some system is chosen to be the prime quarry; Roman law after the rediscovery of the *Corpus Juris Civilis*, the French *Code Civil* after its promulgation. The principal reason for the choice of quarry is that its law is accessible because it is written down. This law will also be more elaborated (because it has to provide an answer) and will have the *general* admiration of the lawyers. The full appropriateness of the particular foreign rule for the borrowing system will not then be investigated: it is usually enough that the foreign rule is not obviously and seriously inappropriate. That does not mean that such a foreign rule will inevitably be borrowed or be borrowed without alteration, but only that within the legal tradition there exists a strong predisposition in favor of borrowing and, at that, from the individual preselected system.[3]

A revolution may occur in law or in society. With revolution in law, the legal tradition continues but with appropriate modifications: the basis of the law has been changed. With revolution in society the aim must also be to revolutionize law. The legal tradition is then replaced by another legal tradition in whole or in part.

Law, then, despite its practical impact, is above all and primarily the culture of the lawyers and especially of the lawmakers—that is, of those lawyers who, whether as legislators, jurists, or judges, have control of the accepted mechanisms of legal change. Legal development is determined by their culture; and social, economic, and political factors impinge on legal development only through their consciousness. This consciousness results from the lawmakers' being members of the society and sharing its values and experiences, though of course they are members with a particular standing. Sometimes this consciousness is heightened by extreme pressures from other members of the society, but always the lawmakers' response is conditioned by the legal tradition: by their learning, expertise, and knowledge of law, domestic and foreign.

This book has been both descriptive and explicative; but I should like to conclude with a message. The theme of this book (as of others I have written, though now I go further) is that law is largely autonomous and not shaped by societal needs; though legal institutions will not exist without corresponding social institutions, law evolves from the legal tradition. To understand law in society one must be fully aware of the impact of the legal tradition. Whether, for reform of the law in the future, the impact of the legal tradition can be reduced is very doubtful. But the message is that for satisfactory law in society one must have a satisfactory legal tradition. The main thrust of law reform must be to ensure that the means of making law are the best possible for the society. In this context specific, abiding—indeed natural—features of the culture deserve express mention. Law is treated as existing in its own right: it is being in conformity with lawness that makes law law. Hence, first the means of creating law, the sources of law, come to be regarded as a given, almost as something sacrosanct, and change in these even when they are obviously deeply flawed is extremely difficult to achieve.[4] Secondly, law has to be justified in its own terms; hence authority has to be sought and found.[5] That authority (in some form, which may be perverted) must already exist; hence law is typically backward-looking. These two features make law inherently conservative.[6]

Appendix:
About the Illustrations

The illustrations are taken from a luxury ninth-century Carolingian manuscript, BN lat. 4404, and their context throws a fascinating light on legal evolution, the legal tradition, and legal transplants.

Modern writers on late Roman or early Germanic law and editors of legal texts have the habit—hallowed now for centuries—of keeping apart Roman works such as the *Lex Romana Burgundionum* and Germanic works such as the *Lex Salica*. The former but not the latter, for instance, appears in the standard collections of Roman legal texts along with such works as the *Institutes* of Gaius. And the Germanic codes are published in their own collections. This is highly misleading. The early manuscripts which were functional, whether as school books or handbooks for magnates, contain items from each group, according to need.[1] Students and judges deciding a case all wanted to find in their manuscript the legal rules appropriate to the persons involved. It is obvious that, in practice, cross-fertilization could easily occur under the Carolingians.

BN lat. 4404, for example, contains the *Breviarium Alaricianum*, the Merovingian version of the *Lex Salica*, a text of the *Lex Alemannorum*, and another of the *Lex Ribuaria*. A later note by Etienne Baluze declares that the manuscript originated in Gallia Narbonensis. The illustrations in the present book stand in the manuscript at the beginning of the *Breviarium;* similarly, at the beginning of the *Lex Alemannorum* is a full-page portrait of Lodhanri, king and duke of the Alemanni.

The *Breviarium Alaricianum* is a composite work with texts drawn from Roman imperial enactments (*leges*) and juristic texts (*ius*). The *leges* are a very abridged version of the *Codex Theodosianus,* the *Novellae* of Valentian III, Majorian, Marcian, and Severus, plus imperial constitutions from the unofficial *Codex Gregorianus* and an extract from the equally unofficial *Codex Hermogenianus.* The juristic texts are the *Epitome* of Gaius, the *Sententiae* of Paul, and a fragment from the *Responsa* of Papinian. Again misleadingly, the *Breviarium Alaricianum* does not appear along with the *Lex Romana Burgundionum* in the collections of Roman legal texts; but the *Epitome Gai* and the *Sententiae Pauli* do, and these works, whether they are by Gaius and Paul or are postclassical epitomes, have survived only through the Visigothic codification. The Visigoths have transmitted this portion of classical culture to us. It was above all in this form, moreover, that Roman law was known before the Reception and helped to prepare the ground for the acceptance of the *Corpus Juris Civilis.*

The manuscript, quite typically then, illustrates a progression: from classical Roman law to Roman law for the Roman subjects of the Visigoths to Roman law for the Gallo-Roman inhabitants of Gallia Narbonensis, side by side with law for Germanic inhabitants, and so on to the Reception. The Roman texts in BN lat. 4404 are frequently marked by symbols to direct attention to them, but these are lacking from the Germanic texts. Thus, it would appear likely that the bulk of the population was Gallo-Roman. The fact that Lodhanri is illustrated with such respect leads Rosamond McKitterick to suggest that the magnate for whom the manuscript was copied could have been an Alemannian.[2]

The first illustration, at the beginning of the *Breviarium* on fol. 1v, shows Theodosius II carrying his code, with Valentinian III and two other anonymous legislators (but presumably intended to be Majorian and Marcian). The facing page, fol. 2r, has in the top left quarter a figure designated as Severus, who is presumably the Emperior Libius Severus (461–65), of whom one constitution is included in the *Breviarium*. The top right corner portrays the jurist Gaius, the bottom left Paul, and the bottom right Hermogenianus. These, to my knowledge, are the earliest portraits of Roman jurists.

Notes

I. The Roman System of Contracts and the Legal Tradition

1. A discussion of the nature of legal ideas is postponed to the beginning of Chapter 3; but the theoretically minded reader may wish to refer to it now.

2. See Glanvil (d. 1190), *Tractatus de Legibus et Consuetudinibus Regni Anglie* 10.18f.; A.W.B. Simpson, *A History of the Common Law of Contract* (Oxford: Clarendon Press, 1975), p. 4.

3. For the argument see A. Watson, *Legal Transplants: An Approach to Comparative Law* (Edinburgh: Scottish Academic Press; Charlottesville: University Press of Virginia, 1974), p. 15.

4. *Mancipatio* was a formal ceremony needed to transfer certain important kinds of property; its obligational content was an inherent warranty against the eviction of the transferee from the property. *Nexum*, though obscure, was probably a variant form of mancipatio; it involved a creditor's having real rights over the person of the *nexus:* see M. Kaser, *Das römische Privatrecht*, 2d ed., 1 (Munich: Beck, 1971): 165ff.; A. Watson, *Rome of the XII Tables* (Princeton: Princeton University Press, 1975), pp. 11ff., 134ff.; Gy. Diósdi, *Contract in Roman Law* (Budapest: Akadémiai Kiadó, 1981), pp. 30ff. It is Diósdi who would add *in iure cessio* as involving an obligation. This was a fictitious lawsuit to effect the transfer of ownership in which the defendant, the owner, put up no defense to a claim of owner-

ship from the plaintiff, the transferee. None of these three institutions had a major impact on the later development of the law of contract.

5. See, e.g., J.A.C. Thomas, *A Textbook of Roman Law* (Amsterdam: North-Holland, 1976), p. 226.

6. *Rhetorica ad Herennium* 2.13.19.

7. See M. Kaser, *Das altrömische Ius* (Göttingen: Vandenhoek & Ruprecht, 1949), pp. 256ff.; H. van den Brink, *Ius Fasque: Opmerkungen over de Dualiteit van het archaïsch-romeins Recht* (Amsterdam: Hakkert, 1968), pp. 172ff.; O. Behrends, *Der Zwölftafelprozess* (Göttingen: Schwartz, 1974), pp. 35f.; and the authors they cite.

8. Kaser, *Privatrecht*, 1:168ff.

9. Ibid., pp. 170f.

10. See for the argument A. Watson, *Roman Private Law around 200 B.C.* (Edinburgh: Edinburgh University Press, 1971), pp. 126f.

11. The *condictio furtiva*, which is exceptional, need not concern us here.

12. Kaser, *Privatrecht*, 1:492f.

13. In French law any noncommercial (in the technical sense) transaction above a very small amount can be proved only by a notarial act or a private signed writing except, under article 1348 of the *Code Civil*, when it is not possible for the creditor to procure writing. "Possible" here refers to moral possibility as well as physical, and in certain close relationships—such as, at times, those involving one's mother, mistress, or physician—the obtaining of a writing is regarded as morally impossible.

14. Some scholars—e.g., Kaser, *Ius*, p. 286—suggest that a real action, the *legis actio sacramento in rem*, was available for mutuum before the introduction of the condictio. There is no evidence for this, and the availability of such an action would make it more difficult to explain the introduction of the condictio. But the suggestion would not adversely affect the idea expressed here that mutuum was given specific protection because the arrangement was among friends and stipulatio was morally inappropriate. At whatever date, a commercial loan would involve interest, a stipulatio would be taken, and there would be no need for specific legal protection of mutuum.

15. D. Daube, "Money and Justiciability," *Zeitschrift der Savigny-Stif-*

tung (rom. Abt.) 92 (1979): p. 1ff., 11; see earlier D. Daube, "The Self-Understood in Legal History," *Juridical Review* 18 (1973): 129f.

16. *Collatio* 10.7.11. The action has often been thought to be something other than an action for deposit or to be an action for what was later called *depositum miserabile*, but see Watson, *Private Law*, p. 151, and Kaser, *Privatrecht* 1:160, n. 49.

17. E.g., Watson, *Private Law*, p. 157; Kaser, *Privatrecht*, 1:160.

18. E.g., Kaser, *Privatrecht*, 1:160.

19. O. Lenel, *Das Edictum Perpetuum*, 3d ed. (Leipzig: Tauchnitz, 1927), pp. 288f. Praetors were elected public officials who, among other things, had control over particular courts. They had no power to legislate, but in practice they modified the law enormously by issuing edicts setting out actions they would give and special defenses they would allow.

20. The literature is enormous, but see, e.g., W. Litewski, "Studien zum sogenannten 'depositum necessarium,' " *Studia et Documenta Historiae et Iuris* 43 (1977): 188ff., esp. 194ff., and the works he cites.

21. Gy. Diósdi, *Contract*, pp. 44f.

22. See A. Watson, *Law of Obligations in the Later Roman Republic* (Oxford: Clarendon Press, 1965), pp. 40ff.

23. See Kaser, *Privatrecht* 1:546; H. F. Jolowicz and B. Nicholas, *Historical Introduction to the Study of Roman Law*, 3d ed. (Cambridge: Cambridge University Press, 1972), pp. 288ff.; and the works they cite.

24. Th. Mommsen, "Die römischen Anfänge von Kauf and Miethe," *Zeitschrift der Savigny-Stiftung* (rom. Abt.) 6 (1885): 260ff.

25. Scholars who take any one of these approaches—especially the first two—also wish to give a central role in the invention to the peregrine praetor. This seems to me to be unnecessary, but the point need not detain us here: see A. Watson, *Law Making in the Later Roman Republic* (Oxford: Clarendon Press, 1974), pp. 63ff.

26. This appears even in Mommsen, "Anfänge," p. 260; see also E. I. Bekker, *Die Aktionen des römischen Privatrechts*, 1 (Berlin: Vahlen, 1871): 156ff.; V. Arangio-Ruiz, *La Compravendita in diritto romano*, 2d ed., 1 (Naples: Jovene, 1956): 57ff. Diósdi objects, asking why it would be necessary to cut up "the uniform contract of spot transactions into two separate contracts, to confirm the two promises

with a *stipulatio,* then abandon the *stipulationes* shortly so that at the beginning of the preclassical age the contract appears as already in its classical shape." *Contract,* p. 45. By "spot transaction," he appears to have *mancipatio* in mind. There are two flaws in this argument. First, the object of the sale-type transaction would not always be a *res mancipi,* in which case *mancipatio* would be inappropriate. Secondly, even in the earliest times, even when the object was a *res mancipi,* the parties would not always want a spot transaction, but delivery at a later time, and *mancipatio* would not then be used.

27. A. Watson, "The Origins of Consensual Sale: A Hypothesis," *Tijdschrift voor Rechtsgeschiedenis* 32 (1964): 245ff.

28. In fact, the stipulatio could not be taken from a son or slave with full protection until the introduction of the *actio quod iussu.* That action appears to be based on an edict of the praetor (Lenel, *Edictum,* p. 278), and actions based on an edictal clause giving the plaintiff a new right of action cannot be safely dated earlier than ca. 100 B.C.: see Watson, *Law Making,* p. 38.

29. B. Nicholas does not agree, and suggests for the persistence of the stipulations that they imposed strict liability, whereas liability on sale would be based only on good faith: Jolowicz and Nicholas, *Introduction,* p. 289, n. 8 (at p. 290). This does not address the problem, which is not the continued use of stipulatio but the absence of implied warranties in sale. Those who wanted strict liability could still have demanded a stipulatio even if *emptio venditio* had implied warranties (which could be excluded). Again, this approach does not lessen the commercial inconvenience of the lack of implied warranties. Moreover, it must be surprising in a contract of sale based on good faith that there is no warranty of title or of quiet possession.

30. Strict textual proof is lacking, but a development from the strict law stipulatio to good faith *emptio venditio* can have been no other.

31. For this, see A. Watson, *The Making of the Civil Law* (Cambridge: Harvard University Press, 1981), pp. 14ff.

32. The impact of the defects in early consensual sale would be less noticeable, of course, where what was sold was a *res mancipi* and it actually was delivered by *mancipatio,* which did have an inherent

warranty against eviction. Even here, however, there was no warranty against latent defects.

33. For views see, e.g., Jolowicz and Nicholas, *Introduction*, pp. 294ff. Significantly, one recent writer on ancient hire, H. Kaufman, offers no view on the origins of the consensual contract: see *Die alt-römische Miete* (Cologne: Böhlau, 1964).

34. Actually, locatio conductio is so obviously a residual category—every bilateral transaction involving a money prestation that is not sale is hire—that one need not start with the assumption of the priority of sale. From the very fact of the residual nature of hire one can deduce the priority of sale. Unless, that is, one were to argue (as I think no one would) that originally sale transactions were within the sphere of *locatio conductio* and that *emptio venditio* was carved out of this all-embracing contract.

35. *Rhetorica ad Herennium* 2.13.19. See A. Watson, *Contract of Mandate in Roman Law* (Oxford: Clarendon Press, 1961), p. 22.

36. K. Visky, *Geistige Arbeit und die Artes Liberales in den Quellen des römischen Rechts* (Budapest: Akadémiai Kiadó, 1977), pp. 146ff.

37. Watson, *Law Making*, pp. 31ff., esp. p. 38.

38. See, e.g., Lenel, *Edictum*, pp. 254ff., who thinks there was such an action; and Kaser, *Privatrecht*, 1:537, who apparently tends to think there was not.

39. Watson, *Obligations*, pp. 182ff.

40. Though the *actio quod iussu* is not evidenced for the Republic: see Watson, *Obligations*, pp. 187f.

41. A further reason for the introduction of the new contractual action was that it could allow more of a role for reliance on good faith, even though the praetorian action did not have a condemnation clause framed *ex fide bona*. In favor of this explanation is the fact that *fiducia*—the older form of real security (and not contractual in terms of the definition given at the beginning of this chapter)—was erected by using mancipatio with a special clause relating to trust and faith; see Watson, *Obligations*, pp. 172ff. Indeed, it is possible that the existence of fiducia was influential by way of analogy for the creation of pignus. Fiducia had two limitations: its dependence on mancipatio meant that only *res mancipi* could be so pledged (unless the cumbrous *in iure cessio* were used), and that only citizens

(or those with *commercium*) could be creditors or debtors. The praetor might thus have introduced the very different contract of pignus, also because of the difficulties involved in framing stipulations that would adequately cover the debtor's rights.

42. Thomas, *Textbook,* pp. 267ff.

43. Watson, *Obligations,* pp. 21ff.

44. See, above all, A. Watson, "Consensual *societas* between Romans and the Introduction of *formulae,*" *Revue Internationale des Droits de l'Antiquité* 9 (1962): 431ff.

45. D.17.2.29.pr., 1: see A. Watson, "The Notion of Equivalence of Contractual Obligation and Classical Roman Partnership," *Law Quarterly Review* 97 (1981): 275ff.

46. *Laesio enormis* is postclassical, whether it is to be attributed to Diocletian or Justinian: C.4.44.2; 4.44.8.

47. G.3.159; D.17.1.12.16. That damages were doubled for breach in *depositum miserabile* is not a problem. Depositum miserabile could still be subjected to special regulation.

48. D.45.1.122; 45.1.126.2; 45.1.140.pr. There is something illogical in accepting a written document as evidence of a stipulatio. It can show the intention of the parties, but scarcely that they went through the formalities.

49. D. M. MacDowell, *The Law in Classical Athens* (Ithaca: Cornell University Press, 1978), p. 233.

50. M. Crawford, *Roman Republican Coinage* (Cambridge: Cambridge University Press, 1976), pp. 35ff.

51. The state of development of barter before the time of Justinian is very obscure, much disputed, and need not be gone into here. For literature, see, e.g., Thomas, *Textbook,* pp. 312f., and Kaser, *Privatrecht* 1:381.

52. D. Daube, "Three Quotations from Homer in D.18.1.1.1," *Cambridge Law Journal* 10 (1949): 213ff.

53. A relatively satisfactory outcome, I believe, from the Sabinian viewpoint would be that barter is sale, and both parties have the obligations of sellers.

54. Daube, "Money," pp. 8, 9.

55. For these see Watson, *Obligations,* p. 257.

56. The literature is immense, since authors often have to take a position, but see, e.g., R. Yaron, "Semitic Elements in Early Rome,"

in *Daube Noster*, ed. A. Watson (Edinburgh: Scottish Academic Press, 1974), pp. 343ff.; Watson, *Law Making*, pp. 186ff.

57. See A. Watson, *Sources of Law, Legal Change, and Ambiguity* (Philadelphia: University of Pennsylvania Press, 1984).

58. See J. M. Manresa, *Commentarios al Código civil español*, 2d ed., 1 (Madrid: Revista de Legislación, 1903): 545f.; Vélez Sarsfield's note on the Argentinian *Código civil*, art. 325; K. Zweigert and H. Kötz, *Introduction to Comparative Law* trans. T. Weir, 1 (Amsterdam: North Holland, 1977): 123ff.

59. Title 7, arts. 30–33. Cf. *Las Siete Partidas*, 4.19.5, 7; 6.13.8; *Leyes de Toro*, 10, 11; *Leyes de Recopilación*, 5.8.8.

60. Arts. 227–29.

61. *Digest*, title 7, art. 30: Code of 1825, art. 221.

62. Zweigert and Kötz, *Introduction*, 1:126.

63. Livre 1, art. 10. In his *Rapport*, p. 6, Cambacérès writes: "Il faut bannir de la législation française l'odieuse recherche de la paternité," and he describes the fact of conception as "couvert d'un voile impénetrable." I have not been able to see his first "projet" of 1793.

64. See Fenet, *Recueil complet des travaux préparatoires du Code Civil*, 10 (Paris: Ducessois, 1836): 154.

65. Reported in the anonymous (but by the Baron Favard de Langlade) *Conférence du code civil avec la discussion particulière du Conseil d'état et du Tribunat* (Paris: Firmin Didot, an XIII [1805]), p. liv.

66. P. D. King, "King Chindaswind and the First Territorial Law-Code of the Visigothic Kingdom," in *Visigothic Spain*, ed. E. James (Oxford: Clarendon Press, 1980), p. 131.

67. A particularly striking example of the creation of law for reasons other than the obviously societal is to be found in the bold but superbly argued thesis of Calum Carmichael in *Women, Law, and the Genesis Traditions* (Edinburgh: Edinburgh University Press, 1979). He claims: "The source of the problems taken up in the Deuteronomic legislation is not, as is almost universally thought, matters that arose in the every-day life of the Israelites at various times and places, but matters that are found in the literary tradition available to the legislator in his time" (p. 5). "Certain laws in the Deuteronomic legislation are about many of the women we meet in the book of Genesis" (p. 1).

68. Examples of legal development which seem absurd to those not

steeped in the law abound. I have chosen those here because I have not used them before. But see also, e.g., A. Watson, *Society and Legal Change* (Edinburgh: Scottish Academic Press, 1977).

69. D.47.2.21.pr. (Ulpian). The text actually says that the action will be for the value of what was taken, but that answer, as modern scholars agree, is either that of Ulpian or of Justinian's compilers. It cannot have been the original position or the question would not have been worth discussing.

70. Or, perhaps, "preferable."

71. All this is conclusive against J.A.C. Thomas's explanation of the attitude of Ulpian in D.47.2.21.pr. He says: "For Ulpian, though one might 'contrectate' the whole thing, one contrectated *lucri faciendi causa* [with the intention of making a gain]—and thus committed *furtum* of—only what was in fact removed." Thomas, "Digest 47.2.21," in *Synteleia Arangio-Ruiz* (Naples: Jovene, 1964), 2:610. But this would mean that Ulpian had found a solution to the problem, and paragraph 5 establishes that he had not. His contemporary Paul in D.47.2.22.1 may have found a general solution (along the lines postulated by Thomas for Ulpian), but it is just as likely that his solution is for one particular type of situation.

72. J. C. Gray, *The Rule Against Perpetuities,* 4th ed., by R. Gray (Boston: Little, Brown, 1942), p. 191.

73. See, above all, ibid., pp. 126ff.; W. Holdsworth, *History of English Law,* 2d ed., 7 (London: Methuen, 1937): 81ff., 193ff.; A.W.B. Simpson, *Introduction to the History of the Land Law* (Oxford: Oxford University Press, 1961), pp. 208ff.

74. 3 Ch. Cas. 1.

75. (1736) Cas. t. Talb. 228.

76. (1799) 4 Ves. 227; (1805) 11 Ves 112.

77. (1833) 1 Cl. & Fin. 372.

78. In my fourth year of teaching Real Property at Oxford, I asked Dr. John Morris, co-author of one of the most famous books on the subject, if I might work through with my students some problems that he had prepared for his students. With his usual generosity of spirit he agreed. A few days later I received an even kinder letter from him setting out the answers to the problem. I was not at all insulted by the notion that I could not reason through the puzzles on my own.

79. See for these, e.g., J.H.C. Morris and W. Barton Leach, *The Rule Against Perpetuities*, 2d ed. (London: Stevens, 1962); Cheshire and Burn's *Modern Law of Real Property*, 13th ed., by E. H. Burn (London: Butterworths, 1982), pp. 294ff.

80. Morris and Leach, *Rule*, p. 18.

81. Ibid., pp. viii and 18.

82. Painvin v. Deschamps, Cour de cassation, Chambre civile, 19 July 1870, *Dalloz* 1870, jurisp. p. 361. Here we need look only at the courts, though juristic debate was lively. For an excellent treatment in English, with quotation of the sources, see A. T. von Mehren and J. R. Gordley, *The Civil Law System*, 2d ed. (Boston: Little, Brown, 1977), pp. 590ff. All the cases cited here are discussed by them.

83. Guissez, Cousin et Oriolle v. Teffaine, Cour de cassation, Chambre civile, 16 June 1896, *Dalloz*, 1897, jurisp. p. 433.

84. Chemins de Fer de l'Ouest v. Marcault, Cour de cassation, Chambre civile, 21 January 1919, *Dalloz* 1922, jurisp. p. 25.

85. Compagnie Française des Tramways Electriques et Omnibus de Bordeaux v. Chemins de Fer du Midi, Cour de cassation, Chambre civil, 16 November 1920, *Dalloz* 1920, jurisp. p. 169.

86. See Bessières v. Compagnie des Voitures l'Abeille, Cour de cassation, Chambre civil, 29 July 1924, *Dalloz* 1925, jurisp. p. 5; Jand'heur v. Les Galeries Belfortaises, Cour de cassation, Chambres réunies, 13 February 1930, *Dalloz* 1930, jurisp. p. 57.

87. *Dalloz* 1930, 1, p. 59.

88. But discussion of fault keeps creeping back.

89. See Dame Briday v. de Cela, Tribunal de grande instance de Lyon, *Semaine Juridique et Juris-Classeur Périodique* 2:16822.

90. Taupin v. Arrachepied, Cour de cassation, Chambre civile, 5 March 1947, *Dalloz* 1947, jurisp. 296.

91. Jand'heur v. Les Galeries Belfortaises: quoted by von Mehren and Gordley, *Civil Law System*, p. 631.

92. See, above all, Watson, *Sources of Law*, and A. Watson, "Legal Change: Sources of Law and Legal Culture," *University of Pennsylvania Law Review* 131 (1983): 1121ff., esp. from p. 1151. Although the fact need not be stressed here, the nature of the sources of law available to the lawmakers has a profound impact on the course of legal change in any given society.

II. Customary Law

1. For the development of a theory of custom in Roman law, insofar as there is one, see D. Nörr, "Zur Entstehung der gewohnheitsrechtlichen Theorie," in *Festschrift für W. Felgentraeger* (Göttingen: Schwartz, 1969), pp. 353ff. A very different view of the formation of customary rules, particularly in international law, is given by J. Finnis, *Natural Law and Natural Rights* (Oxford: Clarendon Press, 1980), pp. 238ff. Custom as a source of international law is not discussed in this chapter.

2. It is presumably on this account that Rudolf von Jhering described custom as the "pet" of the German Historical School: see *Geist des römischen Rechts* 2.1, 5th ed. (Leipzig: Breitkopf & Härtel, 1894), p. 29.

3. But this chapter is not directly an essay on the history of legal theory, and I have done little more than read the appropriate pages in the Gloss and typical authors such as Oinotomus, Wesembecius, J. Voet, Vinnius, and Heineccius.

4. K.C.W. Klötzer, *Versuch eines Beytrags zur Revision der Theorie von Gewohnheitsrecht* (Jena: Mauke, 1813), esp. pp. 189ff.; S. Brie, *Die Lehre von Gewohnheitsrecht*, vol. 1 (Breslau: Marcus, 1899).

5. I have translated this quotation from K. Larenz, *Methodenlehre der Rechtswissenschaft*, 2d ed. (Berlin: Springer, 1969), p. 338; see also his *Allgemeiner Teil des deutschen Bürgerlichen Rechts: Ein Lehrbuch*, 5th ed. (Munich: Beck, 1980), p. 10. In later editions Larenz is much less explicit, though he seems to have basically the same opinion: see *Methodenlehre*, 4th ed. (1979), pp. 345ff. He expressly adopts the view of Nörr that the theory of customary law, as such, is unsatisfactory.

6. F. von Savigny, *System des heutigen Römischen Rechts* (Berlin: Veit, 1840), 1:174f.

7. D.1.3.39. And this view is generally accepted within the tradition.

8. No comparison can be drawn with desuetude of statute, for which there is no need for a belief that the contrary acting is in accord with the law.

9. See, e.g., the remarks of C. K. Allen, *Law in the Making*, 7th ed. (Oxford: Clarendon Press, 1964), p. 136.

10. Savigny, *System*, 1:171.

11. Ibid., pp. 175f.

12. See, e.g., Allen, *Law in the Making*, pp. 87ff. Yet, oddly, it survives indirectly, without the theoretical trappings, in a number of writers; for instance, add to the authors quoted in A. Watson, *Society and Legal Change* (Edinburgh: Scottish Academic Press, 1976), pp. 1f, L. M. Friedman, *A History of American Law* (New York: Simon & Schuster, 1973), p. 595. In a curious way G. Calabresi seems a modern distortion mirror of Savigny, and for him the judges (like jurists) "represent" the people at one remove, the current "legal landscape" generally reflects popular desires, and legislation inhibits law from giving the people what they want and need: *A Common Law for the Age of Statutes* (Cambridge: Harvard University Press, 1982).

13. J. Austin, *Province of Jurisprudence Determined* (London: Weidenfeld & Nicolson, 1954), pp. 30ff., 163ff.; Austin, *Lectures on Jurisprudence*, 2 (London: John Murray, 1863): 222ff.

14. But J. C. Gray argues that statutes are not law but only sources of law, because their meaning is declared by the courts, and *"it is with the meaning declared by the courts, and with no other meaning that they are imposed upon the community as law."* The Nature and Sources of Law, 2d ed., by R. Gray (New York: MacMillan, 1927), p. 170.

15. Allen, *Law in the Making*, p. 70.

16. J. A. Brutails, *La Coutume d'Andorre* (Paris: Leroux, 1904), p. 55.

17. Ibid., pp. 47ff.

18. Ibid., p. 342; P. Ourliac, ed., *La jurisprudence civile d'Andorre: Arrêts du tribunal supérieur de Perpignan; 1947-1970* (Andorra: Editorial Casal i Vall, 1972), p. 12, n. 7.

19. Further reports appear in subsequent volumes.

20. C. Obiols i Taberner, *Jurisprudéncia civil andorrana: Jutjat d'apellacions; 1945-1966* (Andorra: Editorial Casal i Vall, 1969).

21. A. Watson, *Sources of Law, Legal Change, and Ambiguity* (Philadelphia: University of Pennsylvania Press, 1983), pp. 45f.

22. Ibid., pp. 46f.

23. But not all contemporaries saw borrowing of a neighbor's custom as borrowing it as and to be the custom of the borrower: see the preface of Guy Coquille (d. 1603) to his *Coutume de Nivernais*.

24. Of course, none of this is to be taken as meaning that it is not also often the case that the customary law does derive from preceding

local behavior. But even where this is so, there are great difficulties in regarding opinio necessitatis as providing the factor that turns behavior into law, as is discussed later in this chapter.

25. Austin, *Province*, p. 31.
26. *In quattuor libros Institutionum Imperialium Commentarius*, ad 1.2.7.
27. It may be worth mentioning in this connection that the Bavarian civil code of 1756, *Codex Maximilianeus Bavaricus Civilis*, 1.2. sec. 15, expressly requires for customary law both the will of the people and the consent of the ruler.
28. A. Watson, *The Nature of Law* (Edinburgh: Edinburgh University Press, 1977), p. 3.
29. F. Pollok and F. W. Maitland, *History of English Law*, 2d ed., by S. F. C. Milsom, 2 (Cambridge: Cambridge University Press, 1968): 399f.
30. For this practice see Watson, *Sources of Law*, pp. 31ff.
31. Ibid., pp. 28ff.
32. Ibid., pp. 47ff.
33. F. Tomás y Valiente, *Manual de historia del derecho español*, 4th ed. (Madrid: tecnos, 1983), p. 133.
34. Certainly the compilers of unofficial collections of customary law frequently praise the quality and the descent from their forefathers. But we cannot generalize from these writers. They wrote these works because they were attached to the customs, but this does not imply the same feeling in other members of the community. Indeed, the authors often lament that the customs are not being kept.
35. An *Oberhof* was the *Schöffen* of another place selected as a mother town, who gave replies on points of law submitted to them.
36. Watson, *Sources of Law*, pp. 37f.
37. Ibid., pp. 42f. With time, the use of the *enquête par tourbes* became more complicated.
38. J. F. Holleman, *Shona Customary Law* (London: Oxford University Press, 1952), p. x.
39. It is common for authorities on customary law to regard their law as ancient: see Watson, *Sources of Law*, pp. 44f.
40. L. Shapera, *Handbook of Tswana Law and Custom*, 2d ed. (London: Cass, 1965), pp. 39f.
41. F. A. Ajayi, "The Judicial Development of Customary Law in Nigeria," in *Integration of Customary and Modern Legal Systems in*

Africa, ed. The Law Faculty, University of Ife (Ife-Ife, Nigeria: University of Ife Press, 1971), p. 126.

42. Hans Cory, *Sukuma Law and Custom* (London: Oxford University Press, 1953), p. vii.

43. But see, e.g., A.N.A. Allott, *Essays in African Law* (London: Butterworth, 1960) pp. 3ff., and *New Essays in African Law* (London: Butterworth, 1970), pp. 9ff.

44. See also, for instance, the volumes of *Restatement of African Law* by various authors, under the general editorship of A.N.A. Allott, for the School of Oriental and African Studies, University of London, and published by Sweet & Maxwell, London.

45. See above all, Cory, *Sukuma Law*, p. xiii f.

III. The Cause of the Reception of Roman Law

1. P. Vingradoff, *Roman Law in Medieval Europe*, 3d ed. with preface by F. De Zulueta (Oxford: Oxford University Press, 1961), p. 11.

2. It is possible for a society to adopt a law of slavery—by borrowing for instance—before it has slaves. But the societal wanting of slaves still comes before the desire for the law.

3. This is the definition of law that I proposed in my *Nature of Law* (Edinburgh: Edinburgh University Press, 1977). It is appropriate to restate it here, but the present argument would not be affected by its excision.

4. In the last few paragraphs I have been stressing the courts and the judges for the emergence of a standard, since I am adopting the traditional hypothesis that law at first emerges from individual decisions rather than from general commands of the political sovereign. But if the standard were thought to be established by a general command and applied through the courts, then an exactly parallel argument could be constructed.

5. At this stage I wish to use the term *lawyers* very loosely to include, for instance, legislators, not all of whom have legal training.

6. E.g., my *Sources of Law, Legal Change, and Ambiguity* (Philadelphia: University of Pennsylvania Press, 1984) and "Legal Change: Sources of Law and Legal Culture," *University of Pennsylvania Law Review* 131 (1983): 1121ff.

7. See, for an outline, K. Zweigert and H. Kötz, *Introduction to Comparative Law*, trans. T. Weir, 1 (Amsterdam: North Holland, 1977): 89ff.

8. A. Watson, *Society and Legal Change* (Edinburgh: Scottish Academic Press, 1977), pp. 107ff.

9. Watson, *Source of Law*, pp. 25ff., 70ff.

10. "Feudal Laws" here refers to the *Libri Feudorum* and the commentaries on them.

11. See, e.g., G. Vismara, esp. *Edictum Theoderici*, in *Ius Romanum Medii Aevi*, part I, 2 b *aa* α (Milan: Giuffré, 1967); H. J. Becker, s.v. *Edictum Theoderici* in *Handwörterbuch zur Deutschen Rechtsgeschichte*, 1 (Berlin: Schmidt, 1971): 802ff.; H. Schlosser, *Grundzüge der neueren Privatrechtsgeschichte*, 4th ed. (Heidelberg: Müller, 1982), p. 6.

12. A. D'Ors, *Estudios visigóticos II: El código de Eurico* (Rome and Madrid: Consejo Superior de Investigaciones Cientifices, Delegacion de Roma, 1960), p. 8; E. Levy, *Zeitschrift der Savigny-Stiftung* (rom Abt.) 79 (1962): 479.

13. "Leges Theudosianas calcans Theudoricianasque proponens." *Epist.* 2.1.3.

14. Other contenders for the honor of authorship of the *Edictum Theoderici* have been Odovaker (476–93) and the Burgundian Gundobad (472–516).

15. Vismara, *Edictum*, p. 29. The problem, of course, is one of jurisdiction: to this we will return.

16. Provision 32 speaks only of barbarians, but its purpose seems to be to give those who are soldiers of the state the same rights of testation that Romans had. I do not understand Vismara's comment (*Edictum*, p. 61), that a few provisions—especially 34, 43, and 44—are specifically for Romans or barbarians. These apply expressly to both peoples.

17. An edition such as that of J. Baviera lists for the provisions the corresponding Roman law texts: Baviera, *Fontes Iuris Romani Antejustiniani*, 2 (Florence: Barberá, 1940): 684ff.; and see Vismara, *Edictum*, pp. 127ff.

18. See, e.g., E. Levy, "The First 'Reception' of Roman Law in Germanic States," *American Historical Review* 48 (1942): 22.

19. Lord Stair, *The Institutions of the Law of Scotland*, 1st ed. (1681), 1.1.15.

20. In practice these edicts changed the law enormously.

21. C. Calisse in *General Survey of Events &c. in Continental Legal History* by various authors (Boston: Little, Brown, 1912), p. 51; H. Conrad, *Deutsche Rechtsgeschichte,* 2d ed., 1 (Karlsruhe: Müller, 1962): 59; d'Ors, *Estudios II,* p. 4; F. Tomás y Valiente, *Manual de historia del derecho español,* 4th ed. (Madrid: tecnos, 1983); p. 102. Schlosser puts the *Codex* just before the fall: *Grundzüge,* p. 6.

22. *Cod. Paris. lat.* 12161; for this see H. Brunner, *Deutsche Rechtsgeschichte,* 2d ed., 1 (Leipzig: Duncker & Humblot, 1906): 482f. It is published in *Monumenta Germaniae Historica, Leges,* 1 (Hanover: Hahn, 1902): 3ff.

23. D'Ors, *Estudios II.*

24. Calisse, *General Survey;* K. F. Drew, *The Burgundian Code* (Philadelphia: University of Pennsylvania Press, 1949), p. 6.

25. See, e.g., Tomás y Valiente, *Manual,* p. 103; R. McKitterick, "Some Carolingian Law-Books and Their Function," in *Authority and Power: Studies on Medieval Law and Government,* ed. B. Tierney and P. Linehan (Cambridge: Cambridge University Press, 1980), pp. 13ff.; and, above all, J. Gaudemet, *Le Breviaire d'Alaric et les Epitome,* in *Ius Romanum Medii Aevi,* part 1, 2b *aa* β (Milan: Giuffré, 1965). Editions of these epitomes are to be found in G. Hänel, *Lex romana visigothorum* (reprint; Aalen: Scientia, 1962).

26. A. García Gallo, "Nacionalidad y territorialidad del derecho en la epoca visigoda," *Anuario de Historia del Derecho Español* 13 (1941): 168ff.

27. See the bibliography in Tomás y Valiente, *Manual,* p. 110. García Gallo has modified his opinion.

28. E.g., Tomás y Valiente, *Manual,* p. 107.

29. García Gallo, "Nacionalidad," p. 194; d'Ors, *Estudios II,* pp. 6ff.

30. See also P. D. King, "King Chindaswind and the First Territorial Law-Code of the Visigothic Kingdom," in *Visigothic Spain,* ed. E. James (Oxford: Clarendon Press, 1980), pp. 131ff, and King's unpublished Cambridge Ph.D. thesis.

31. See P. Merêa, *Estudos de direito visigótico* (Coimbra: Da universidade, 1948) pp. 199ff.; quoted by Tomás y Valiente, *Manual,* p. 107.

32. F. C. von Savigny, *Geschichte des Römischen Rechts im Mittelalter,* 2d ed. 2 (Heidelberg: Mohr, 1834): 73ff.

33. Ibid., pp. 77ff. Not all editions of the Visigothic Code have the same

numbering of the texts. For the convenience of the nonspecialist reader I have in the citations that follow adopted that of S. P. Scott, *Visigothic Code* (Boston: Boston Book Co., 1910).

34. On degrees of relationship: *L. Visigoth.* 4.1, taken from *Pauli Sententiae* 4.11. On legitimate defense: *L. Visigoth.* 8.1.2., taken from the *interpretatio* to *C.Th.* 4.22.3. On interest: *L. Visigoth.* 5.5.8–9, taken from the *interpretatio* to *C.Th.* 2.33.1–2.

35. *L. Visigoth.* 4.3.3. The rule is in *C.Th.* 3.17.4.

36. *L. Visigoth.* 5.7.2., taken from *C.Th.* 4.7.1.

37. A. Esmein, *Cours élémentaire d'histoire du droit français,* 14th ed., by R. Genestal (Paris: Sirey, 1921), p. 35.

38. In the heading the name Gundobad is usual, but one manuscript has Sigismond.

39. It is sometimes said that there are references in the code to earlier Burgundian legislation, for instance in title 18.1: see, e.g., Drew, *Burgundian Code,* pp. 8f. But the wording in the text could as easily refer to a law (relating to horses) which has not come down to us but may be the law referred to in title 49.4 and be the work of Gundobad.

40. "Qui formam et expositionem legum conscriptam, qualiter iudicent, se noverint accepturos, ut per ignorantiam se nullus excuset." Sec. 8. But some provisions of the *Lex Gundobada* are made to apply to Romans also: e.g., 4.1; 4.3; 4.4; 6.3; 6.9.

41. *L. Burg.* 77.1. For this paragraph to this point see, above all, Savigny, *Geschichte,* 2:5ff.

42. The *interpretatio* to *C.Th.* 3.8.2, 3 in title 24.1; to *C.Th.* 3.16.1 in 34.3.

43. O. Stobbe, *Geschichte der deutschen Rechtsquellen* (reprint; Aalen: Scientia, 1965), 1:110.

44. Thus, *L. Burg.* 4.6. = *L. Visigoth.* 8.4.1; *L. Burg.* 4.7 = *Roth.* 340, *Lex Sal.* 23; *L. Burg.* 4.8 = *L. Visigoth.* 8.4.9; *L. Burg.* 6.1, 3 and 20.2 = *L. Visigoth.* 9.1.14; *L. Burg.* 6.4.9 = *L. Visigoth.* 9.1.5; *L. Burg.* 23.4 = *L. Visigoth.* 8.5.1, *Roth.* 349; *L. Burg.* 25.1, 27.7, and 103.1 = *Lex Baiuw.* 9.12 (cf *L. Visigoth.* 8.3.2. and *Lex Sal.* 27.6); *L. Burg.* 27.1–2 = *L. Visigoth.* 8.3.10, *Lex Sal.* 9, *Roth.* 344; *L. Burg.* 39.1–2 = *L. Visigoth.* 9.1.3 and 9.1.6; *L. Burg.* 68 = *L. Visigoth.* 3.4.4., *Lex Baiuw.* 8.1, *Roth.* 212; *L. Burg.* 72 = *L. Visigoth.* 8.4.23; *L. Burg.* 73.1–2 = *L. Visigoth.* 8.4.15; *L. Burg.* 73.3 = *L. Visigoth.* 8.4.3, *Lex Sal.* 38.8, *Roth.* 338, 341.

Code. Paris lat. 12161 has been identified with part of the *Codex Euricianus,* and of it we should pair cap. 320 with *L. Burg.* 14; cap. 277 with *L. Burg.* 17.1 and 79.5; cap. 305 with *L. Burg.* 1.3. For this and for the whole account of the *Lex Burgundionum* see, above all, Brunner, *Rechtsgeschichte,* 1:497ff.

45. See, e.g., H. Maine, *Ancient Law,* chap. 8 (Everyman edition [London: Dent], pp. 174f.); E. Levy, "Reflections on the First 'Reception' of Roman Law in Germanic States," in *Gesammelte Schriften,* 1 (Cologne: Böhlau, 1963): 201ff.

46. See the very just remarks of E. Levy, "The Reception of Highly Developed Legal Systems by Peoples of Different Cultures," in *Schriften,* 1:210ff., esp. pp. 217ff. Furlani's edition of the *Lex Romana Burgundionum,* in *Fontes Iuris Romani Antejustiniani,* 2:714ff., gives cross-references to the Roman sources.

47. See, e.g., Tomás y Valiente, *Manual,* pp. 108ff.

48. *Manual,* p. 99: Tomás y Valiente relies heavily on Ramón d'Abadal i de Vinyals, "Del reino do Tolosa al reino de Toledo," *Discusso de ingreso en la R.A.H.* (Madrid, 1960).

49. E. N. van Kleffens, *Hispanic Law until the End of the Middle Ages* (Edinburgh: Edinburgh University Press, 1968), p. 80.

50. For what follows see, above all, Tomás y Valiente, *Manual,* pp. 126ff.

51. For a full, if dated, account of the early history of the Bologna Law School, see Hastings Rashdall, *The Universities of Europe in the Middle Ages,* 2d ed., by F. M. Powicke and A. B. Emden (London: Oxford University Press, 1936), pp. 87 ff. See also S. Kuttner, "The Revival of Jurisprudence," in *Renaissance and Renewal in the Twelfth Century* ed. R. L. Benson and G. Constable (Cambridge: Harvard University Press, 1982), pp. 299ff.

52. A. Watson, *Legal Transplants: An Approach to Comparative Law* (Edinburgh: Scottish Academic Press; Charlottesville: University Press of Virginia, 1974).

53. Ibid., pp. 57ff., 88ff.

54. Watson, *Sources of Law,* pp. 28ff.

55. K. Zweigert and H. Kötz, *Introduction to Comparative Law,* trans. T. Weir, 1 (Amsterdam: North-Holland, 1977): 89ff.

56. Watson, *Legal Transplants,* pp. 93f. The phenomenon need not be confined to the spread of law. David Daube suggests that Judaism (especially, I think he means, in its proselytizing form of Chris-

tianity) owes much of its attraction from the beginning of the current era to its possession of written books. "It is consistent with this explanation" he says, "that Jewish-Christian preaching has had scant success in the East—India, China—with comprehensive Scriptures of its own." And he adds in parentheses, "In my opinion, the predominance of Roman law from the Middle Ages on owes more to its availability in a written corpus than to quality." *Ancient Jewish Law* (Leiden: Brill, 1981), p. 11. And see, for the transmission of parables in the early Christian tradition, J. Jeremias, *The Parables of Jesus*, rev. ed. (London: S.C.M. Press, 1963), pp. 33ff.

57. Tomás y Valiente, *Manual*, pp. 180ff. My friend Michael Hoeflich tells me that he believes Justinian's *Code* was known, but not widely.

58. Though the prestige might be in part the general or political prestige or power of the state that created the law, such as ancient Rome or Napoleon's France.

59. Calisse, *General Survey*, pp. 39f., esp. p. 40, n. 1.

60. "In illis autem regionibus, in quibus secundum legem Romanam iudicentur iudicia, iuxta ipsam legem committentes talia iudicentur; quia super illam legem vel contra ipsam legam nec antecessores nostri quodcumque capitulum statuerunt nec nos aliquid constituimus." *Edictum pistense*, cap. 20, in *Monumenta Germaniae Historica, legum sectio* 2, 2:319.

IV. Evolution and Revolution

1. Sir George Mackenzie, *Works*, 1 (Edinburgh, 1716): 24f. (of his Pleadings).

2. See Lord Stair, *The Institutions of the Law of Scotland*, 2d ed. (1693), 1.1.10, 16; cf. G. Mackenzie, *The Institutions of the Law of Scotland*, 1st ed. (1684), 1.1.

3. In the first edition, of 1681, Stair appears to give more weight to a single decision than he does subsequently. Mackenzie observes that though the Lords of Session may depart from their own previous decision it is not their habit to do so: *Institutions*, 1.1.

4. Stair expressly lists feudal law as carrying weight, and here he is thinking of feudal law not previously accepted as part of Scots law.

Stair also considers rules of Roman law once accepted into the law of Scotland as becoming part of Scots customary law.

5. The reference should be to book 43, not 53, of the *Digest*.
6. Sir James Balfour of Pittendreich, *Practicks*, 2 (Edinburgh: Stair Society, 1963): 544.
7. James Craig, *Ius feudale*, 2.8.15 (2.8.7, in the Leipzig edition of 1716). This work was first published in 1655, but had been written half a century before.
8. David Hume, *Lectures*, ed. G.C.H. Paton, 4 (Edinburgh: Stair Society, 1955): 245f.
9. Stair, *Institutions*, 1.6.36ff.
10. See, e.g., J. Erskine, *Institute of the Law of Scotland*, 1st ed. (1773), 2.1.2.
11. Stair, *Institutions* (2d ed.), 2.7.8. (The equivalent, almost identical passage in the first edition is 1.17.8.)
12. Erskine, *Institute*, 1.2.1.
13. See D.39.3: cf. A. Watson, *The Law of Property in the Later Roman Republic* (Oxford: Clarendon Press, 1968), pp. 155ff.
14. See the reconstruction of the *formula* in O. Lenel, *Das Edictum perpetuum*, 3d ed. (Leipzig: Tauchnitz, 1927), p. 375.
15. Hume, *Lectures*, ed. Paton, 3 (1952): 209.
16. Ibid., p. 225.
17. G. J. Bell, *Principles of the Law of Scotland*, 10th ed., by W. Guthrie (Edinburgh: Clark, 1899), p. 399. But see earlier A. McDouall (Bankton), *An Institute of the Laws of Scotland*, 1 (Edinburgh, 1751), p. 682.
18. Erskine, *Institute*, 2.1.2.
19. The further argument of the pursuers that there were particular restrictions by statute on an owner's use, and Mackenzie's reply need not detain us.

From D.39.3.3.pr. one might argue that in the Roman republic at least, some jurists would give the *actio aquae pluviae arcendae* when water was polluted. But the law is not clear.

20. J. Rankine, *The Law of Land-Ownership in Scotland*, 4th ed. (Edinburgh: Green, 1909), p. 564.
21. Bell, *Principles*, p. 434; cf. T. B. Smith, *Scotland: The Development of Its Law and Constitution* (London: Stevens, 1962), p. 528.

22. A. Watson, *The Making of the Civil Law* (Cambridge: Harvard University Press, 1981), pp. 83ff.

23. Case law that formed a custom shows the step-by-step way in which Roman law directly entered a mature system of law that was theoretically largely based on custom. But Roman law could also indirectly enter a system of law by being incorporated into a juristic book, from which it might gradually penetrate that system: see, e.g., ibid., esp. pp. 53ff. Or it could be incorporated in statute.

24. See K. Zweigert and H. Kötz, *Introduction to Comparative Law*, trans. T. Weir, 1 (Amsterdam: North Holland, 1977): 138, 156ff.; Watson, *Making of the Civil Law*, pp. 104ff.

25. See the preface, secs. 15–23, of the *Project des Corpus juris Fredericiani*, or *Code Frédéric* (1749–51), quoted in part by A. Watson, *Sources of Law: Legal Change and Ambiguity* (Philadelphia: University of Pennsylvania Press, 1984), pp. 64f.

26. Watson, *Making of the Civil Law*, pp. 99ff.

27. Zweigert and Kötz, *Introduction*, 1:89ff.

28. Watson, *Making of the Civil Law*, passim, but esp. pp. 1ff.

29. We need not, I think, be more precise.

30. Zweigert and Kötz, *Introduction*, 1:30ff.; R. David and J.E.C. Brierly, *Major Legal Systems in the World Today*, 2d ed. (London: Stevens, 1978), pp. 151f.

31. E. L. Johnson, *Introduction to the Soviet Legal System* (London: Methuen, 1969), p. 3. Compare W. E. Butler, *Soviet Law* (London: Butterworths, 1983), pp. 1ff, 24f, 164ff.

32. David and Brierly, *Systems*, pp. 143ff.; Zweigert and Kötz, *Introduction*, 1:293ff.

33. David and Brierly, *Systems*, p. 183; cf. p. 25.

34. Zweigert and Kötz, *Introduction*, 1:309.

35. One example may stand for many: Ataturk's acceptance of Swiss law as the law of Turkey in 1926. For a long time there was great doubt as to whether the imposition, especially of civil marriage and especially in rural Turkey, had taken. See above all the papers in *Annales de la Faculté de Droit d'Istambul*, vol. 6 (1956): F. Ayiter, "The Interpretation of a National System of Laws Received from Abroad," p. 43; H. Z. Ülken, "Le droit coutumier et le code civil," pp. 88ff.; H. V. Velidedeoğlu, "De certains problèmes provenant de

la réception du code civil suisse en Turquie, pp. 111ff. See also O. Kahn-Freund, "Uses and Misuses of Comparative Law," *Modern Law Review* 37 (1974): 16f. By 1973, marriages registered legally amounted to 78% in communities under 2,000 souls, and well above 90% in larger communities: see W. F. Weicker, *The Modernisation of Turkey* (New York: Holmes & Meier, 1981), p. 56. For the very powerful impact of Western law now on rural Turkey, but also the survival of traditional law, see J. Starr, *Dispute and Settlement in Rural Turkey* (Leiden: Brill, 1978), esp. pp. 275ff.

The case of the imposition of a state's law on a conquered territory need not be separately discussed: it is a composite of the other situations, especially of two, three, and four.

36. In this context it is entirely unsurprising that so often the initiative comes from someone outside of the legal tradition: see A. Watson, "Legal Change: Sources of Law and Legal Culture," *University of Pennsylvania Law Review* 131 (1983):1156.

V. Conclusions

1. I would not agree, but this is not the place for a discussion.
2. See A. Watson, *Sources of Law: Legal Change and Ambiguity* (Philadelphia: University of Pennsylvania Press, 1984).
3. For this paragraph see also A. Watson, *Legal Transplants: An Approach to Comparative Law* (Edinburgh: Scottish Academic Press; Charlottesville: University Press of Virginia, 1974).
4. See Watson, *Sources of Law*.
5. See Watson, *Legal Transplants*, pp. 57ff., 88ff.
6. This does not mean there are not radical lawyers. But except when they are legislators, they are "bad" lawyers—not in an ethical sense, but in the sense that they have to use arguments outside the reach of the accepted mode of legal reasoning. They therefore appear to the generality of lawyers to be at the intellectual mercy of the traditionalists. Pointing this out is in no sense to be construed as support for conservative positions. In fact, precisely because of the force of the legal tradition, legal change is frequently the result of efforts of nonlawyers or of lawyers outside the tradition.

Appendix: About the Illustrations

1. See, R. McKitterick, "Some Carolingian Law-Books and Their Function," in *Authority and Power: Studies in Medieval Law and Government,* ed. B. Tierney and P. Linehan (Cambridge: Cambridge University Press, 1980), pp. 13ff., and the works she cites.
2. Ibid., p. 21.

Glossary

actio aquae pluviae arcendae The Roman action against a neighbor whose work might change the flow of rainwater in a way that might cause damage on the plaintiff's land.

actio certae pecuniae The Roman action available to recover a sum of money that had been lent.

actio quod iussu The Roman action against a head of household in respect of a contract made by his slave or son on his authorization.

advocate The Scottish equivalent of the English barrister. In both countries the legal profession is split, and the advocate or barrister specializes in litigation.

capitularies Royal legislation under the Carolingians.

cas fortuit In French law "chance," which operates as a defense when injury has been caused.

cause étrangère In French law an "external cause" that can not be imputed to a defendant and excuses him from liability for damage to person or property.

commodatum The Roman contract of loan for use.

condictio The Roman action in which a nonowner claimed that the owner of something was under a legal obligation to deliver it to him.

contractatio The physical element, wrongful handling, which was needed to constitute theft in Roman law.

Corpus Juris Civilis The name given since the seventeenth century to Justinian's codification of Roman law and his subsequent enactments.

damnum infectum In Roman law, damage not yet done but threatening as a result of a neighbor's defective property.

delict The Roman equivalent of a tort. In French law a delict is a deliberate, not negligent, wrong.

depositum The Roman contract of deposit.

depositum miserabile Roman deposit made following a shipwreck, fire, earthquake, or collapse of a house.

Edict The setting down by a high elected Roman public official of the rules he would follow in carrying out his office. The individual clauses are usually written as "edicts." The most important Edicts for us were those of the praetors, who had control of the law courts.

emptio venditio The Roman contract of sale.

enquête par tourbes A method in medieval France to establish the existence of a custom that was not known to the judge.

ercto non cito The oldest form of partnership at Rome. When a head of family died, all those subject to his power who became free of power on his death were partners in the inheritance until it was divided.

exceptio A clause of defense inserted into the Roman *formula* by which a defendant did not deny the plaintiff's pleadings but claimed some other fact had to be taken into account.

fiducia A Roman form of security of *res mancipi* in which ownership was transferred to the creditor.

force majeure In French law "force" which cannot be foreseen or averted and operates as a defense for damage to person or property.

formula The pleadings in an action in classical Roman law.

furtum Theft in Roman law, which was treated primarily as a private wrong, not a crime.

in iure cessio A Roman method of transferring property, using a fictitious lawsuit. The defendant owner put up no defense, and the thing was adjudged to the plaintiff.

interdict An order issued by an authorized official to prohibit someone from a particular course of conduct.

laesio enormis In late Roman law a ground for setting aside a sale of land if the agreed price was less than one-half the land's value.

legis actio The archaic form of Roman procedure.

legis actio per condictionem The archaic form of the Roman *condictio*.

legis actio per iudicis postulationem An archaic form of Roman procedure in which a judge was appointed immediately after the assertion and denial of the claim.

legis actio sacramento in rem Archaic Roman procedure claiming property in which an oath was sworn on the validity of the claim, and the action proceeded on whether the oath was justly sworn.

locatio conductio The Roman contract of hire.

mancipatio A formal method of transferring ownership of *res mancipi*.

mandatum A Roman contract in which one person agreed to do something gratuitously for another.

mutuum The Roman contract of loan for consumption. The borrower's obligation was to return an equivalent.

nexum An institution related to *mancipatio* in which a free person became bound to another on account of loan or debt.

Oberhof The Schöffen of a town who gave rulings on points of law submitted from other towns. Despite the name, the Oberhof—except that of Lübeck—did not function as a court giving binding decisions.

pays de droit coutumier Territories in medieval northern France where the law was primarily custom.

pays de droit écrit Territories in medieval southern France where Justinian's codification was regarded as the primary law, supplemented by local custom and later legislation.

permutatio The Roman contract of barter.

pignus The main Roman form of real security and the relevant contract.

praetor The second highest elected Roman official, whose duties included control over courts.

Proculians One of the two main schools of law in ancient Rome. Despite numerous attempts, no convincing theory has been advanced for the basis of their differences with the Sabinians.

prodigal A person determined as a spendthrift and allowed only restricted dealings with his property.

quasi-delicts In French law, torts committed by negligence, and not deliberately.

res mancipi Types of property regarded as of particular importance in early Rome and transferrable only by a formal method.

Sabinians One of the two main schools of law in ancient Rome. See "Proculians," above.

Schöffen Nonprofessional judge-jurists of medieval Germany.

servitude An easement.

societas The Roman contract of partnership.

stillicide The right to allow water to drip onto a neighbor's land.

stipulatio A Roman contract formed by oral question-and-answer which could be used for any type of transaction.

sui heredes Those persons at Rome who became independent of any person's paternal power on the death of the ancestor in question.

Weistümer Collections setting out the law of a German village.

Index

About the Author

Alan Watson is Nicholas F. Gallicchio Professor of Law and the Director of the Center for Advanced Studies in Legal History at the University of Pennsylvania. He is author of numerous books, including *Law Making in the Later Roman Republic, Rome of the Twelve Tables, Legal Transplants,* and *The Making of the Civil Law.*